The Murder Factory:
Life and Work of H. H. Holmes,
First American Serial Killer

Alexandra Midal

**The Murder Factory:
Life and Work
of H. H. Holmes,
First American
Serial Killer**

SternbergPress

Contents

Introduction:
Design and Serial Killing

It will be remembered that the remains of a large kiln made of fire brick was found in the Castle basement. It had been built under Mr. Warner's supervision for the purpose of exhibiting his patents. [...] It was into this kiln that I induced Mr. Warner to go with me, under pretense of wishing certain minute explanations of the process, and then stepping outside, as he believed to get some tools. I closed the door and turned on both the oil and steam to their full extent. In a short time not even the bones of my victim remained.[1]

It was in these terms that the United States' first serial killer, Herman Webster Mudgett, better known as Henry Howard Holmes, confessed to one of the countless crimes he had committed by strangulation, asphyxiation, cremation, and various other means in the house he had designed for these very purposes. While the newspapers attributed several hundred murders and disappearances to him, the exact number of his victims cannot be established with certainty. Indeed, some of the people Holmes claimed to have killed, such as his janitor Robert Latimer, appeared in flesh during his trial (their identity could be established thanks to their birth certificates). Holmes was a serial killer, as well as a patent liar and a con man, whose career in crime betrays a sound understanding of the technologies of his time—the era of late nineteenth-century industrial capitalism. In 1896, aged thirty-five, Holmes, the man with multiple identities, was sentenced to death and hanged, taking many of his secrets, inventions, and lies with him to his grave.

Just ten years earlier, Holmes had acquired a patch of land he had been coveting for a while. Although not a professional architect, he drew up the plans for his future home and supervised its construction down to the smallest detail. His construction was so vast that neighbors called it the Castle.[2] Few would have guessed, though, that behind its stylish facade, the house boasted some of the most advanced domestic furnishings of its day, including a dumbwaiter, a human-sized furnace, and a wall-to-wall remote-controlled gas and electricity system. The ultimate rational-mechanical setting for homely murder mysteries, Holmes's building partakes in the literal realization of the modernist-functionalist project as formalized by Nikolaus Pevsner in *Pioneers of the Modern Movement* and by Sigfried Giedion in *Mechanization Takes Command*.[3] Published in 1936, Pevsner's book links the origins of the modern movement to the emergence of the machine. Its explicit subtitle—*From William Morris to Walter Gropius*—defines the boundaries of this historical study, in which the author argues that, "Morris laid the foundation of the modern style; with Gropius, its character was ultimately determined."[4] Starting his genealogy with British utilitarianism and ending it with German functionalism, Pevsner posits a unitary conception of the origins of modernity that begins with design and the British Industrial Revolution, not with architecture. The figure of Holmes, it appears, occupies a counter position to Pevsner's homogeneous, linear succession of virtuous and heroic "pioneers." But is Holmes any closer to Giedion's *Mechanization*, which adopts a radically different perspective? Giedion defines the modern movement through detailed considerations on such varied topics as locks, bathtubs, breadmaking, and Chicago's slaughterhouses. His encyclopedic project maps the relationships between technological achievements on the one hand, and social and cultural evolutions on the other. This approach leads him to argue in favor of a history of aesthetic and mechanical innovation in the triumphant perspective of progress. While both texts establish a system of references for the architecture of the modern movement, they also lay the foundations of design history as a field of study, merging modernism with functionalism.

8

It is from this perspective that Holmes's activities should be read. At once lethal, practical, and convenient, his Castle contained nearly one hundred rooms, apartments, and retail storefronts. His architectural feat is firmly rooted in the functionalist project, while questioning the project and its limits. It would be naive to consider the inception of the industrial revolution in the United States and the almost simultaneous emergence of the serial killer as a mere coincidence. The present investigation reaches beyond society's morbid fascination with lurid crime stories and instead examines Holmes's architectural achievement not only as a functionalist paradigm that fits in perfectly with the perspective of modern mechanization and its implementation, but also as a manifestation of seriality at the crossroads of the assembly line and the emergence of the concept of the "serial killer."[5] Far from being a coincidental appearance, Holmes was the product of a convergence of rationales through which two seemingly antagonistic practices were united by one common denominator: the new industrial modes of production, of which design and serial murder are but two different manifestations. The joint emergence of these concepts suggests a triangular relationship between the conception of human life, seriality (and its corollaries), and the human psyche challenged by modernity. This shift in perspective is not without consequences.

With *The Jungle*, Upton Sinclair was the first novelist to describe the inhumane working conditions in Chicago's slaughterhouses.[6] Thirty years later, in 1936, Charlie Chaplin depicted in *Modern Times* the hallucinations of a worker struggling with a single repetitive task: over and over, he must perform the same gesture on the short stretch of the assembly line to which he has been assigned. And surely it is no coincidence that after having illustrated the excesses of industrialization through the figure of an exploited and exhausted worker, Chaplin played *Monsieur Verdoux* (1947), the serial killer famously inspired by Henri Désiré Landru. The French murderer and con man, working as a clerk in an architect's office, had initially tried his luck at peddling a proto-motorbike of his own invention. But after collecting the first installments from his clients, he and his *pétrolettes* conveniently disappeared. Beginning 1909, Landru changed his modus operandi, placing matrimonial ads in newspapers with the aim of seducing wealthy widows, which he proceeded to strip of their fortune and murder before returning to his wife and child. He is thought to have arranged 283 meetings and murdered eleven women, ten in his villa in Gambais, on the outskirts of Paris.

Chaplin used the story of Landru to expose the actions of a man who treats women as if they were objects, subjecting them to a system of economic circulation based on consumption, disappearance, and profit-making. Chaplin captured the monstrous dimension of the murderer according to the blueprint established a few years earlier by Holmes, who adopted the rational, efficient principles of industrialized livestock processing to commit his murders and cash in on his victims' life or property insurances, stocks, and inheritances. Much like his predecessor across the Atlantic, Landru, pursuing the same mercantile objective, did not distinguish between the animate and the inanimate. Both killers went about their macabre business in the private sphere of the home, which they saw as an instrument of capital at the service of personal enrichment. As Mark Seltzer, the author of *Serial Killers: Death and Life in America's Wound Culture*, explains, the interior of the house becomes "absolutely crucial in understanding cases of repetitive violence" as a characteristic of mass modernity, which makes no noticeable distinction between repetition, standardization, efficiency, and murder. Holmes carries out these operations at an unprecedented scale and with a formidable sense of functionality.

The aim of this book, therefore, is not to examine Holmes's acts—in the vein of the famous studies conducted by the nineteenth-century Italian criminologist Cesare Lombroso—as the hidden doings of an exceptionally intelligent pervert, the manifestations of a pathological drive, or the acts of a neuropath caused by madness, criminal impetus, or genius. Each of these categories would imply situating him in the extraterritorial realm of illness, and consequently in a form of disempowerment and abnormality that would exclude him from the artistic field I propose to examine. On the contrary, Holmes's case points to a territory beyond the *malaria urbana* of the modern movement,[8] taking part a dynamic of rationality and efficiency that is symptomatic of the shift operated by the industrial revolution and its handling of all things living. This shift was described by Holmes's contemporary, the engineer Thomas Edison, in the following terms: "Problems in human engineering will receive during the coming years the same genius and attention which the nineteenth century gave to the more material forms of engineering."[9] The present case study, whose main protagonist lives and works in a smart house *avant la lettre* situated in the birthplace of modern industry, a stone's throw from the world's most sophisticated slaughterhouses, will allow us to grasp the importance of this economic, mechanical, and cultural transformation.

[1] "The Confession of H. H. Holmes," *Philadelphia Inquirer*, April 12, 1896, reprinted in Dimas Estrada, ed., *The Strange Case of Dr. H. H. Holmes* (Los Angeles: Waterfront Editions, 2005), 347.

[2] "It is impossible to say who first christened the building with its byname. Perhaps it was a neighborhood resident, paying tribute to the imposing look of Holmes's creation. Or perhaps it was Holmes himself, whose talent for self-promotion matched his grandiose ambitions. Whatever the case, soon after its completion, Englewood's citizens began referring to the new building as 'the Castle.'" Harold Schechter, *Depraved: The Shocking True Story of America's First Serial Killer* (New York: Pocket Books, 1994), 35.

[3] Nikolaus Pevsner, *Pioneers of the Modern Movement: From William Morris to Walter Gropius* (London: Faber and Faber, 1936); Sigfried Giedion, *Mechanization Takes Command: A Contribution to Anonymous History* (New York: Oxford University Press, 1948).

[4] Pevsner, 42.

[5] These ideas can also be found in the transformations described by Frederick Winslow Taylor in *The Principles of Scientific Management* (New York: Harper and Brothers, 1911), in which the author identifies the main factors that come into play in productivity: speed, rhythm, tools, human resources, organization, and efficiency.

[6] See Upton Sinclair, *The Jungle* (Clayton, DE: Prestwick House, 2005). First published in serial form in the socialist newspaper *Appeal to Reason* between February and November 1905, the book revealed the exploitative working conditions in Chicago's mechanized slaughterhouses. It had such an impact on a wide readership that it prompted protest actions, eventually bringing about change for workers' rights.

[7] Mark Seltzer, *Serial Killers: Death and Life in America's Wound Culture* (New York: Routledge, 1998), 203.

[8] The term was coined for a new kind of disease diagnosed in the nineteenth century and refers to "functional disorders caused by prolonged stays in big cities." See Honoré Bourguignon, "Quelques réflexions sur la 'malaria urbana', ou sur les troubles fonctionnels produits par le séjour prolongé dans les grandes villes," *L'Union médicale* 10 (June 11, 1861): 210.

[9] Thomas Edison, letter printed on the cover of *Engineering Magazine* 53 (January 1917). Quoted in Meyer Bloomfield, "The New Foremanship: Relation of Foremen to the Working Force," reprinted in *Selected Articles on Employment Management*, ed. Daniel Bloomfield (New York: H. W. Wilson, 1919), 301.

1.

The Scene of the Crime:
A Place of Invention

"It has to be recognized that, in his ghoulish way, Holmes was as much the exponent of the American dream as Henry Ford or Horatio Alger."[1] The practice of serial killing is deeply linked with the history of industrialization. The proliferation of appliances designed to improve household economy follows the rise of industry at large, echoing the modernization of factory assembly lines and the specialization of tasks. The unprecedented confluence of efficiency and mechanization was made possible by the latter, spreading beyond the production of consumer goods to serve as a model for the slaughtering and dismembering of livestock on the assembly lines of the world's first mechanized meat factories, in Chicago. Against the backdrop of these simultaneous and large-scale developments, this disturbing coincidence appears as an articulation of a world in which the relationship between the animate and inanimate culminates in the reality that no life is spared by the machine and the lure of profit.

The serial character of industrial production finds its most extreme manifestation in Holmes's Castle: "In the story of Holmes and his crimes, there is nothing more interesting than the description of his Castle, where he is accused of having provided all sorts of devices for disposing of his victims. […] It was built with the sole idea of convenience for the commission of crimes," as a contemporary newspaper noted.[2] At the dawn of the nineteenth century, by revisiting and adapting the principles of industrialization to the home, and by combining them with efficiency and functionality, the first serial killer in US history exposed the uncontrollable consequences of mechanization and revealed its dark side.

The nineteenth century in the United States was marked by the invention of devices, tools, and systems derived from industrial manufacturing, which became indispensable instruments in the smooth running of the modern house. Catharine Beecher was a conceptual pioneer in this field, as she conceived the equipment of the house according to hygienist and functionalist principles inferred from her observations of assembly-line work in the mill factories of Lowell, Massachusetts.[3] She invented domestic rationalization, applying the scientific principles of standardization to the household. Beecher envision the house as a functional entity. Mirroring the organization of the factory, she advocated a rationalization of the housewife's tasks with the express goal of saving time and alleviating fatigue. By appropriating the organizational principles of assembly lines and the specialization of tasks in the country's factories, she initiated a revolution. These transformations influenced the experiments of researchers and anonymous users alike, to whom the subtitle of Giedion's book, *A Contribution to Anonymous History*, pays tribute. Holmes's "anonymous contribution" can be situated between these two poles in what Seltzer describes as a profession: "Serial killing, by all accounts, became a career option at the turn of the century."[4]

Holmes plays an important role in the origins and foundations of modern design, which since Pevsner had been interpreted as the galvanization of democratic morality for industrial purposes. By highlighting the extent to which the house had turned into a stage—and if we accept that "the scene of the crime is also the scene of invention"[5]—Holmes's story forms part of a history that reaches beyond a summary distinction between good and bad. Along with Adolf Loos's canonical *Ornament and Crime*, Victor Papanek's "Do-It-Yourself Murder" (which describes designers as a "dangerous breed"), Hal Foster's *Design and Crime* (which uses crime as a discursive form), and the "mean designer" ironically portrayed by Ettore Sottsass, Jr., in "Mi dicono che sono cattivo," Holmes embodies crimes whose motives were laid bare by designer George Nelson during his appearance on CBS's *Camera Three* program.[6]

Preempting the laws of "good design," Holmes conceived a hyperfunctional space in which he could perform all of his brutal activities rationally, conveniently, and quietly. He was so attached to his house and its furnishings that, even as he was fleeing from the police, he was dreaming up a complex of houses based on the model of his Chicago Castle.

Serial Codes and Serial Killers

It was after a several-months-long investigation carried out jointly by Pinkerton's National Detective Agency and the Philadelphia police that H. H. Holmes, the handsome shopkeeper, amateur inventor, and helpful neighbor esteemed by all, was uncovered as a cold-blooded murderer. In the course of the inquiry, they established an initial list of his victims based on unearthed material clues and body parts.

Holmes's first victim was Minnie R. Williams Holmes, a graduate of the Boston Conservatory of Music born in Fort Worth, Texas. Soon after she met Holmes, he hired her as his personal secretary, and they later married. Her sister Nana Williams moved in with the couple soon afterward. A little later, the two sisters disappeared. During a search of the Castle on July 18, 1895, the police recovered rib bones belonging to Minnie.

Investigative work revealed that in 1890 Holmes killed his mistress Julia L. Conner and her eight-year-old daughter Pearl. Conner had been working for Holmes as an accountant when she fell under his spell. She seems to have entrusted him with her savings in the understanding that he would invest them under his own name. A blood-stained piece of clothing was found in her room in the Castle on August 4, 1895. In July 1891, Gertrude Conner, Julia's sister-in-law, was murdered. Her bones were discovered in the cellar of the Castle on July 24, 1895.

In 1892, Holmes lured Emeline Cigrand into working as his personal secretary by offering to pay her an attractive salary. The nineteen-year-old stenographer left her work in Illinois to join him and later became his mistress. She had $20,000 worth of savings in shares. She disappeared in December of the same year, shortly after Holmes had promised to marry her.

On September 23, 1894, Holmes killed Benjamin Pitezel, a chemist who had acted as his accomplice for at least four years. They met in Chicago and seem to have worked together on several occasions. In August 1894, the two men rented a house in East Chicago; later, investigators found Pitezel's body in the living room.

In October 1894, Holmes abducted Alice and Nellie Pitezel, two of his partner's daughters, to Toronto, Canada, where he locked them in a trunk and later gassed them. Their bodies were unearthed on July 15, 1895, by local police detective Alf Cuddy.

A few days later, Holmes strangled their younger brother Howard in a house he had rented for this purpose in Indianapolis. He then proceeded to cut up and burn his body in a furnace.

Holmes's motive was always money. His modus operandi was dictated by the contraptions he stole from inventors who visited his bogus patent office. The scene of his crimes was most often the house he had built on 63rd Street and Wallace, in Englewood. As an architect, designer, and inventor, Holmes was particularly interested in mechanical reproduction, as exemplified by his ABC Copier, a duplicating machine of his own invention akin to a mimeograph.
Holmes's victims were mainly women. Newspapers estimated that he had employed more than one hundred women—and as sources vary widely and many are based on speculation, victim counting is a nearly impossible task. In one of his confessions he admitted to having assassinated thirteen women: Julia L. Connor and her daughter Pearl, a woman named Lizzie, Sara Cook (who was pregnant), Mary Haracamp (a tenant), Emeline Cigrand Rosine van Jassand, Anna Betts, Gertrude Conner, someone he named "Miss Kate," Minnie and Nannie Williams, and Alice and Nellie Pitezel. As noted by Frank Geyer, the Philadelphia police inspector who eventually tracked Holmes down in Boston, all the women with whom Holmes had been romantically involved were blonde. His victims were almost exclusively women, whether his mistresses, employees, and/or accomplices. And the truly remarkable fact is that they all met their tragic fate in the mechanized lair of the Castle.

Holmes's standardized murder practice negated both the individuation of the subject and the singularity of his victims, while engaging with techno-capitalist rationalization. The abstract nature of his victims' dismembered and fragmented bodies, which he often reassembled into skeletons, points to the abstract realm of profit—one where the exploiter is no longer the manufacturer or factory owner, but the killer of women.

Historically, design was founded on a rational homology between manufactured production and household organization, and between economics and functionalism. But a relationship also exists between the treatment of the products of capitalism, whether consumer goods or (women) workers' bodies, and technical rationality pushed to its extremes. Most of Holmes's victims were his employees at the time he murdered them. They were mostly typists (in 1890, nearly 65 percent of typists in the United States were women). This new profession emerged as a consequence of the mechanical reproducibility of writing and the industrial production of typewriters,[7] an invention democratized in 1876 with the launch of the Sholes, Glidden, and Soulé models exhibited by Philo Remington at the Centennial International Exhibition in Philadelphia.[8] Its use required dexterity and speed, two qualities that Remington stereotypically associated with women.[9] Holmes's prey were young women who had left the countryside, attracted by more lucrative propositions than farm work, trying their luck in the prosperous city of Chicago in the late 1880s.

When conducting a body search on Holmes during his arrest in Boston, the police discovered a secret code. To communicate with his accomplices, Holmes had thought up a coding and decoding system based on the word "republican." Written in capitals, the ten letters of the word replaced the letters of the alphabet from A to J; written in lowercase, they represented the next ten letters; the last six letters of the alphabet remained uncoded. The process of encryption and decryption (back then a professional occupation typically held by women) allowed Holmes to securely exchange sensitive information, and points to his wider obsession with duplication and transmission. Holmes embraced modern means of telecommunication, displacing the use of codes from a military context into a domestic sphere that became a stage for the women he victimized. By the nineteenth century, the dismemberment of women's bodies already featured prominently in magic shows. In 1809, the French magician Torrini is said to have premiered a stage number in which he sawed a woman in half, a trick later perfected by P. T. Selbit in the United Kingdom and Horace Goldin in the United States. Holmes dismembered the corpses of his victims in the basement of his house, which he then sold, reassembled, as skeletons to medical schools. In this, he not only got rid of the evidence, but also earned money. "Such a taking apart and reassembly of 'life itself,'" writes Seltzer, "is inseparable from the taxidermic and technophilic exposures of an antinatural and antifeminine violence."[10] Far from being "exquisite," these corpses represent the perpetuation of violence against women and their bodies, particularly in an industrialized country that, notwithstanding its aspiration for progress, reduces women and femininity to the objects of violence. As Seltzer points out, US mass culture is obsessed with combinations of the macabre and technology, its "fascination with spectacles of bodily violence [...] inseparable from the binding of violence to scene, spectacle, and representation: not merely spectacles of sex and violence in public but a sexual violence inseparable from its reproduction and mechanical duplication."[11]

Antihero as Designer

Holmes was not a trained designer, but how else should we define his practice, which combined technology, ingenuity, and serial production? Holmes is as much a counterpoint to the gallery of heroes and geniuses in Pevsner's historical tradition of design as he is to Giedion's history of anonymous inventors. Indeed, both these foundational texts, which have long served as a roadmap for design, neglect the dark side of their discipline's history.

Is Holmes an antihero? The media philosopher Vilém Flusser links design to the idea of deceit. In his view, the designer's skill and alliance with technique is based on "cunning."[12] Flusser refines his argument by examining the etymology of the word "designer": "As a verb ('to design'), meanings include 'to concoct something,' 'to simulate,' 'to draft,' 'to sketch,' 'to fashion,' 'to have designs on something.'" In combination with the machine, design becomes a "device intended to deceive; a lever, for example, cheats gravity, and 'mechanics' is the trick of fooling heavy bodies." In this sense, design is close to the artifice of *technē*. It enslaves its object: "This is the design that is the basis of all culture: to deceive nature by means of technology." Based on the semantics of technology and machine, Flusser questions the traditional *doxa* of design, leaving no doubt that "a designer is a cunning plotter laying his traps."[13] Against the definition of design put forward by the disciples of the modern movement, Flusser casts design as a discipline whose purpose is to deceive nature by means of technology and artifice. His considerations reveal the ingenious nature of the designer as someone capable of grasping the importance of deceit in their work. In doing so, Flusser revolutionizes the concept of functional modern design, undermining the presumed moral foundations on which it was built and making way for the emergence of an alternative story of design that flirts with amorality.

As we know, William Morris, the leading figure of the Arts and Crafts movement, was wary of the consequences of the industrial revolution on working and living conditions in urban behemoths such as London. Holmes, on the contrary, embraced its achievements wholeheartedly. The juxtaposition of these two antagonistic figures—Morris as Dr. Jekyll and Holmes as Mr. Hyde—brings into focus the crucial point of our story: the relationship between morality and progress. Each in their own way, these two contemporaries (who, incidentally, died the same year) put this relationship to the test, the former by exalting it, the latter by exploiting it. Holmes's criminal career questions the foundations of mechanization as profoundly as the virtuous practices of Morris and the Arts and Crafts movement. Highlighting the innate polarity of design, their respective trajectories therefore raise similar issues.

In early editions of the *Guinness Book of Records*, Holmes is listed as the first serial killer in the United States (the category has meanwhile been discontinued, as serial crime is no longer considered a subject worthy of records). His "oeuvre" undermines the sound foundations of conventional design history by inviting us to rethink it from its dark side. Design historian Reyner Banham, in an essay "History and Psychiatry," pointed out the blind spots and denials of the history of modern architecture and accused his predecessors of "amnesia."[14] By appropriating the vocabulary of psychoanalysis to characterize historians' intentional and unintentional omissions, Banham took a distanced view that paved the way for a more nuanced reconstruction of the history of architecture. His concept of a "zone of silence"[15]—a grey area masterfully embodied by the anonymous designer Holmes—further enables us to rethink the history of design. His critique of the conventions of the discipline is all the more powerful as it deconstructs the original misconception of virtuous design. It is therefore around the edges of the epic narrative of design's "pioneers," as Pevsner calls them, that our history of the origins of design—a history at once more complex and more daring—unfolds. It is archetypically embodied by Holmes, whose attention to innovation and industrialization never subsided. Examining the malevolent potential of design through the figure of Holmes and adopting the idea that crime produces an "augmentation in [...] wealth"(to use Karl Marx's terminology)[16] allows us to highlight the ambiguities of a formidably complex yet often simplified discipline. By evoking its horror, we question the virtuousness with which technology was originally associated, if not confused. But more importantly, highlighting its intrinsic toxic potential enables us to shift the central status of functionalism in favor of a new perspective. It remains to be seen if design is strong enough—and nothing is less certain—to finally allow for the integration of these "missing masses,"[17] this accursed share.

To grasp design's instructive potential, it is helpful to pick up on another suggestion by Banham, namely, that "the history of the mechanization of environmental management is a history of extremists, otherwise most of it would never have happened. The fact that many of these extremists were not registered, or otherwise recognized as architects, in no way alters the magnitude of the contribution they have made to the architecture of our time."[18] Holmes is part of a history of paroxysms.

Design and Horror

23   To gauge the importance of these concepts, we must turn our attention to the first design museum: the Museum of Manufactures, in the Marlborough House. Based on the premise of moral education, it was established in London in 1852, with Henry Cole as its inaugural director. Cole sought to make up for the failure of his Great Exhibition of 1851, the first such event that purported to demonstrate the primacy of manufactured products over craftsmanship and their impact on everyday life in the future. Cole also saw the exhibition as an opportunity to celebrate the superiority of British industrial engineering, but much to his despair, nothing went according to plan. While the building in which the exhibition was held— Joseph Paxton's Crystal Palace, the world's first prefabricated glass and iron building, a beacon of technical progress— was a popular and critical success, the manufactured products and artifacts exhibited by the invited nations bore testimony to the prevalence of an outdated ornamental aesthetic and the use of advanced industrial techniques to perpetuate obsolete tastes. Cole was disappointed to see

that, contrary to his hopes, the products on display did not speak in favor of mechanization. Indeed, by celebrating the imitation of antiquated styles, they bore the ostentatious hallmark of bad, bourgeois taste. Far from meeting the organizers' expectations, the Great Exhibition demonstrated that industrialization was no more a token of culture than it was of savoir vivre. Cole's assessment was damning: the industry lacked the necessary guidelines to lead the nation into modernity. To overcome the lack of public enthusiasm for these decorative objects, which contradicted the progressive ideas that industry was supposed to embody, Cole imagined a pedagogical response with which he hoped to give his compatriots the necessary tools for discernment and enable them to refute the cheap aesthetics favored by capitalism. In a bid to instruct his contemporaries in design matters, he founded the Museum of Manufactures. The museum's opening hours, which extended into the late evening, were aimed at drawing in idlers and, more importantly, the working masses. More curiously still, the exhibition in the Marlborough House revolved around the so-called Gallery of False Principles, which visitors had to cross if they wanted to access the rest of the display. By confronting examples of "correct design" and their antithesis, Cole hoped to teach the principles of good taste to a wide audience. Dubbed the "Chamber of Horrors" by the press, the gallery contained eighty-seven "Examples of False Principles in Decoration."[19] Defining a set of rules and specifying for each object the ways in which it failed to abide by them, Cole sought to promote a virtuous dimension of design by means of a dialectical confrontation of artifacts of bad taste with elegant forms that embodied the values of the Victorian era. At the same time, he minimized the impact of World's Fairs which, as Walter Benjamin has shown, turned commodities into deities: "World exhibitions are places of pilgrimage to the commodity fetish. 'Europe is off to view the merchandise,' says [Hippolyte] Taine in 1855."[20] World's Fairs played an important role in the public's fascination with the seductive realm of capitalistic consumer goods.

Inaugurated in January 1852—two months after the end of the Great Exhibition—the Museum of Manufactures represented an attempt to acknowledge this situation. Alas, Cole was once again disappointed by the public reaction. Although the majority of exhibition goers understood the message, many failed to discern good taste from bad—their capacity to pass aesthetic judgments was not helped by the fact that all the objects were displayed indiscriminately on the walls of the museum. Visitors easily confused the rooms, mistaking objects of poor taste for paragons of good design. In 1852, in the weekly journal *Household Worlds*, editor Charles Dickens addressed this problem by publishing a humorous short story by Henry Morley titled "A House Full of Horrors." In it, the author follows a fictional middle-class visitor, Mr. Crumpet, as he discovers the "correct principles of taste." Having heard about the infamous Chamber of Horrors, Crumpet heads straight to the Department of Practical Art, where he is shocked to learn that the pattern of the trousers he is wearing is considered of bad taste. Poor Mr. Crumpet, who thought he was the epitome of elegance. Upon returning home, he is even more distraught: "When I went home, I found that I had been living among horrors up to that hour. […] Horr – horr – horr – hor – ri – ble!"[21] Haunted by this revelatory experience, he no longer knows how to dress or furnish his house. Morley's satire pokes fun at Cole's moral lessons by showing a British public that struggles to perceive design as the expression of industrial authenticity.

The story of the Chamber of Horrors incites us to look at the tensions between good and bad in design from a different angle. Conjuring this horror through Cole's project or, more literally, through Holmes's deeds, implies reassessing the history of design.

[1] Colin Wilson, *A Casebook of Murder* (New York: Cowles Book Company, 1969), 206.

[2] "Holmes Hanged," *The Daily Commercial Herald*, May 8, 1896, 3.

[3] Catharine Beecher published *A Treatise on Domestic Economy for the Use of Young Ladies at Home and at School* (New York: Harper and Brothers, 1841), the first book in a series that included the bestseller *The American Woman's Home* (1896).

[4] Seltzer, *Serial Killers*, 1.

[5] Seltzer, 217.

[6] See Adolf Loos, *Ornament and Crime* (1908; London: Penguin Classics, 2019); Hal Foster, *Design and Crime (And Other Diatribes)* (London: Verso Books, 2002); Ettore Sottsass, Jr., "Mi dicono che sono cattivo" [They Tell Me I'm Mean], *Casabella*, no. 377 (May 1973), reprinted in Ettore Sottsass, Jr., Scritti 1946–2001 (Vincenza: Neri Pozza, 2002), 242–45; and Victor Papanek, "Do-It-Yourself Murder: The Social and Moral Responsibilities of the Designer," in *Design for the Real World: The Social Contribution of Design* (New York: Pantheon Books, 1971), ix. Papanek writes: "There are professions more harmful than industrial design, but only a few of them. And possibly only one profession is phonier. Advertising design, in persuading people to buy things they don't need, with money they don't have, in order to impress others who don't care, is probably the phoniest field in existence today. […] Today, industrial design has put murder on a mass-production basis. By designing criminally unsafe automobiles that kill or maim nearly one million people around the world each year, by creating a whole new species of permanent garbage to clutter up the landscape, and by choosing materials and processes that pollute the air we breathe, designers have become a dangerous breed." George Nelson invited viewers to reflect on the contribution of designers to the production of weapons. The episode was titled "A Problem of Design: How to Kill People" and aired on November 20, 1960. A transcript was published in *Industrial Design* 8, no. 1 (January 1961): 45–53.

[7] See Seltzer, *Serial Killers*, 217.

[8] See Arthur J. Pulos, *American Design Ethic: A History of Industrial Design* (Cambridge, MA: MIT Press, 1983), 181.

[9] Women were considered to be organically dexterous. See Bruce Bliven, Jr., *The Wonderful Writing Machine* (New York: Random House, 1954). See also Juliette C. Kristensen, *Writing Acts: The Rise of Mechanized Writing and the Body of Modernity, 1711–1905* (PhD diss., Kingston University, 2012).

[10] Seltzer, *Serial Killers*, 216.

[11] Seltzer, 129.

[12] Vilém Flusser, "About the Word Design," in *The Shape of Things: A Philosophy of Design*, trans. Anthony Mathews (London: Reaktion Books, 1999), 17.

[13] Flusser, 17, 19.

[14] See Reyner Banham, "History and Psychiatry," *Architectural Review* 127, no. 759 (May 1960): 325–32. Reprinted in Penny Sparke, ed., *Design by Choice* (London: Academy Editions, 1981), 20–22.

[15] Banham, 20.

[16] Karl Marx, "Apologist Conception of the Productivity of All Professions," in *Theories of Surplus Value, Part 1* [1863], trans. Emile Burns, *Capital*, vol. 4 (Moscow: Progress Publishers, 1969), 949.

[17] Bruno Latour, *La clef de Berlin et autres leçons d'un amateur de sciences* (Paris: La Découverte, 1993), 25; my translation.

[18] Reyner Banham, *The Architecture of the Well-Tempered Environment* (Chicago: University of Chicago Press, 1969), 16–17.

[19] See Suga Yasuko, "Designing the Morality of Consumption: 'Chamber of Horrors' at the Museum of Ornamental Art, 1852–53," *Design Issues* 20, no. 4 (2004): 44.

[20] Walter Benjamin, "Paris, the Capital of the Nineteenth Century" [1935], in *Walter Benjamin: Selected Writings, vol. 3, 1935–1938*, trans. Edmund Jephcott et al., ed. Howard Eiland and Michael W. Jennings (Cambridge, MA: Belknap Press, 2002), 36.

[21] Henry Morley, "A House Full of Horrors," *Household Worlds* 4, no. 141 (December 4, 1852): 265–66.

HERMAN WEBSTER MUDGETT

Portraits of Herman Webster Mudgett, alias H. H. Holmes,
albumen print, 1893.

29

alias H. H. Holmes.

HOLMES' "CASTLE"   (63d St., Chicago, Ill.)

Photograph of Holmes's Castle, 1895.

BUILDING IN WHICH HOLMES HAD HIS DRUG STORE.
[Alley way on the left, beneath which gas tank was found.]

Illustration of Holmes's Castle, from "Ribs in the Ashes," *Sunday Times-Herald*, July 21, 1895. Courtesy of the Abraham Lincoln Presidential Library and Museum.

2.

A Rake's Progress:
From Herman Mudgett to
H. H. Holmes

The one thing all witnesses seemed to agree on was Holmes's appearance. He was unanimously described as a well-groomed, well-mannered man who appealed to women. Of average size and build, he had regular features and thick brown hair. He sported a mustache over well-defined lips that contrasted with his pale cheeks and large blue eyes. Although his voice was soft and low, people who met him insisted on his self-assurance and masculinity.

Born on May 16, 1861 in Gilmanton, New Hampshire, to Levi Horton Mudgett, a farmer who worked various odd jobs, and Theodate Page Price, Herman was the third of five children. They were devout Methodists, and Levi is described in many accounts to have been an alcoholic and physically abusive to his wife and children. In the memoirs that he wrote in prison, Holmes recounts an anecdote that he presents as a decisive turn in his nascent criminal personality. On his way to school as a five-year-old boy, he used to walk past the town doctor's office. For young Herman, the place, with its nauseating smells of medications and potions, "was one of peculiar abhorrence."[1] When his schoolmates learned of his fear, they set him up and dragged him into the doctor's office, where they forcefully confronted him "with one of its grinning skeletons which, with its arms outstretched, seemed ready in its turn to seize me."[2] But ultimately, the experience "proved a heroic method of treatment destined ultimately to cure [him] of [his] fears and to inculcate in [him] a strong feeling of curiosity."[3] A true story or ex-post-facto fabrication? In *The Devil in the White City*, Erik Larson muses that, "The incident probably did occur, but with a different choreography. More likely the two older boys discovered that their five-year-old victim did not mind the excursion; that far from struggling and shrieking, he merely gazed at the skeleton with cool appreciation. When his eyes settled back upon his captors, it was they who fled."[4]

Herman's adolescence was divided between work on the family farm in summer and school in winter. A gifted student, he nurtured hopes to leave Gilmanton and attend medical school. At the age of seventeen, he courted a pretty eighteen-year-old blonde, Clara A. Lovering, the daughter of a prosperous citizen of Loudon, New Hampshire. The young couple married secretly in Alton, New Hampshire, on July 4, 1878, and had a child shortly afterward. With the support of his wife, Herman was eventually able to fulfill his dream and began studying medicine at the University of Vermont in Burlington. The following year, in 1882, he transferred to the University of Michigan Medical School at Ann Arbor, before moving to Mooers Fork, New York, where he started practicing medicine in 1884. It was there that the cash-strapped young father, who was constantly looking for ways to earn money, soon committed his first felonies. In order to proceed at ease, he sent his wife and their son Robert back to New Hampshire, promising to join them once he made his fortune. When he was finally alone, he prepared his departure to Chicago.

Herman then began to carry out the first in a series of life-insurance scams, devising a plan that he was to repeat several times over the following years. For this, he asked an accomplice to take out a life insurance policy on him for a stately sum (accounts vary from $12,000 to $40,000, roughly equivalent to between $300,000 and $1,000,000 today). After the first monthly instalments had been paid, his friend suddenly "disappeared." With the help of gravediggers and unscrupulous physicians with whom he had become acquainted during his time as a medical student, Holmes acquired a freshly buried corpse that resembled his missing friend. By slightly doctoring the dead body he was able to fool the authorities and collect the insurance premium. Once reunited, the two accomplices shared the spoils. The trick worked and marked the beginning of his career as a con man.

Holmes Descends on Chicago

Herman had moved to Wilmette, a suburb of Chicago, by 1886, when he opened a modest office as an inventor, under his new pseudonym H. H. Holmes. He eventually settled in Englewood, south of Chicago, where he found a job as a clerk at a drugstore owned by Elizabeth S. Holton. Holton's husband—or so the story goes—was an old man bedridden with terminal prostate cancer. She spent all day at his bedside, soon leaving Holmes in charge of the pharmacy. A few months after the doctor's death, Holmes ran the business himself. To curious neighbors he explained that he had offered the widow to buy the pharmacy through a loan of $100 a month and that, eager to leave town, she had accepted the deal. Mrs. Holton disappeared without saying farewell or leaving the faintest trace, with the exception of a few postcards sent to acquaintances back in Chicago, in which she explained her decision to move back to her family—a con, of course, devised by Holmes to alleviate the neighbors' doubts over the widow's unannounced departure. It worked and, by the end of 1886, Holmes became the owner of the pharmacy.[5] He used his newly gained status to start a career as a polygamist by marrying Myrta Zulique Belknap on January 28, 1887.[6] The young couple moved into an apartment overlooking the pharmacy. In 1889, they had a child, Lucy, but Holmes decided to send them to live with his in-laws in Wilmette. Soon afterward, he sold his store to a young pharmacist from Michigan looking for a place to settle with his wife. They decided to buy the business on the condition that Holmes would not open a pharmacy nearby, to which he agreed.

With the proceeds of the sale, Holmes was able to complete the construction he had started on the vacant lot at the junction of 63rd Street and Wallace, facing the pharmacy. He personally oversaw the construction of what was later dubbed the Castle, built according to plans only he knew. The imposing building held more than one hundred rooms, rooms for tenants, and retail spaces with the most advanced technologies and inventions of their time. The first business Holmes opened in the building was a pharmacy, a flamboyant and grandiose space with brass and copper fittings, stained glass windows, and marble countertops.

Preempting the laws of productive, psychological, and rational functionalism posited by architect Louis Sullivan in 1896 (the year Holmes was executed), Holmes's innovative household devices were concealed behind classic facades punctuated by a succession of turrets.[7] His construction took place in the context of an extensive urban redevelopment scheme after large parts of Chicago were destroyed by the October 1871 fire. As a result, the city, whose buildings had been built mainly from wood, was now riddled with patches of wasteland. As design historian Arthur J. Pulos explains, "It was Chicago, more than New York, that provided the major opportunity for architects and builders to conceive structures that could be erected quickly in a form that was particularly suited to the needs of business."[8] With its reconstruction, the city became a model of urban modernity: "From 1880 to the time of the Columbian Exposition of 1893 the 'Loop' area in Chicago (its business quarter, that is) was the center of architectural development not merely for the United States but for the whole world."[9]

Holmes went about his commercial and criminal activities in the heart of the most densely populated and advanced city in the United States. His businesses were thriving; he was a respected and admired man. Besides the building and the shops on the ground floor, he owned several businesses downtown, including an office from which he promoted his ABC Copier—a duplicating machine that never reached production—as well as a candy store on Milwaukee Avenue run under the name of Frank Wilde, a glass-bending factory in the north of the city, a cigar factory, and apartments in Wrightwood. (He may have owned other commercial interests, but these are the ones that could be ascertained by investigators.)

Thefts, Scams, and Betrayal

Besides these businesses, life-insurance fraud remained Holmes's primary means of income. But although his was a well-rehearsed scheme, it eventually caused his demise. In August 1894, when trying to make the murder of his accomplice Benjamin Pitezel look like a suicide, he mixed up the chemicals; the flawed result aroused the suspicion of the tenacious and diligent Pinkerton detectives hired by the insurance company.

Despite being Holmes's closest and most faithful accomplice, Pitezel himself could not have foreseen this denouement. The two scamsters had been working together for several years, and as in former instances, their latest plan involved taking out life insurance on someone—in this case Pitezel—who would then disappear, only for their dead body to be found and identified a few months later. Pitezel warned his family that they should not be alarmed by his disappearance and that at some point they might be asked to identify the body of a stranger who vaguely looked like him. Then the two men took out a $10,000 policy in Pitezel's name with Fidelity Mutual Life Association, with Holmes paying the first monthly instalments. As part of their plan, they travelled to Mississippi to source a corpse that could be shown to the inspectors mandated by the insurance company, but for reasons unknown, they came back empty handed, prompting Holmes to change plans.

In June 1894, the two men left for Philadelphia, where Pitezel rented an office space on 1316 Callowhill Street (conveniently facing the morgue, as some accounts point out). The plaque on the door read: "B. F. Perry. Patents Bought and Sold." Several days later, on the night of September 3, Pitezel was found dead in the office. His face was disfigured by acid burns, his upper body in a state of advanced decomposition. After a lung autopsy, the coroner's physician concluded that he had been killed by gas inhalation. In order to dispel any doubts about the identity of the corpse and collect the insurance money, Holmes wasted no time and mandated Chicago lawyer Jeptha D. Howe to send a letter to the insurance company in which he stated that the deceased's widow, Carrie A. Pitezel, had confirmed without any doubt that B. F. Perry was indeed her husband. When the insurance company insisted that the body had to be identified by someone who did not belong to the family of the deceased, the widow suggested one of the few acquaintances of her lonely, taciturn husband, an inventor named H. H. Holmes, whom she did not know personally—though she seemed to remember that he had once hired her husband as a chemist.

Holmes immediately set out for Philadelphia to identify Pitezel's body, accompanied by his former accomplice's oldest child, fifteen-year-old Alice. At the morgue, investigators concealed Pitezel's mutilated face from his daughter, only allowing her to glimpse his teeth through a gap in the sheet. Alice was apprehensive, despite having previously been assured by Holmes that the corpse was not her father. She knew the role she was expected to play—to formally identified the corpse. Finally, Holmes mentioned a distinctive sign that lifted any remaining doubt: Pitezel had a wart on his neck. Once it had been found, the identity of the corpse was established. That same afternoon, Holmes called the local office of the insurance company asking to be repaid a $180 debt owed to him by Pitezel, and demanding that the sum be deducted from the total amount due to the widow so that he could be paid immediately.

Why exactly did Holmes then take three of Pitezel's five children—Howard, Nellie, and Alice—to Indianapolis, where he enrolled them in school? Presumably, he was afraid that sooner or later the family would discover the truth and denounce him, and therefore decided to eliminate them. Pressed for time, he managed to convince their mother that she had to leave Chicago with three of her children. A wanted person's notice flagged that the Pinkerton detectives were not fully convinced. In the meantime, Holmes had already left to Irvington, Indiana, where under his pseudonym Howard he rented a modest house for which he bought furniture before disappearing again. It was in the chimney of that house that investigators would later find the charred bones of the young Howard Pitezel.

Holmes then arrived in Detroit, where he set out to prepare the murder of the two Pitezel girls. But as detectives tracked him down, he was forced to change plans again and took them to a house he had rented in Toronto, where he eventually killed them. He then returned to his first wife, Clara, in New Hampshire. Curiously, although she had not heard from her husband since he had moved to Chicago years ago, she seems to have believed Holmes when he explained that his silence was due to a total amnesic breakdown and confinement in a mental institution.

Holmes's tactical retreat was temporary but long enough to attempt yet another homicide—that of Pitezel's widow and her baby—this time operating from a distance using self-made nitroglycerin. After sawing a section of a step of the interior staircase in his home in Burlington, he sent Mrs. Pitezel to fetch a box of important documents from the house. In truth, the box held a flask of explosives, but Mrs. Pitezel and her infant failed to tread on the sawn-off step and thus narrowly escaped death.

In the course of the investigation, detectives discovered that, despite his denials, Holmes had in fact been in Philadelphia the night Benjamin Pitezel was murdered. Detective Frank Geyer, who had been mandated to work with the prosecutor's office, was the first to suspect more than mere fraud and insisted on continuing the investigation on his own, with funding from Fidelity Mutual.[10] From Cincinnati to Indianapolis, Detroit to Toronto, he painstakingly retraced Holmes's movements and, by sheer obstinacy, managed to accumulate damning evidence against him. Meanwhile, thanks to the information collected by Pinkerton, Philadelphia's district attorney George S. Graham had enough material to prosecute Holmes, whose time was clearly running out. On Saturday, November 17, 1894, by order of Chief Inspector Watts, detectives Glidden, Abbott, and McGarr arrested

Holmes in Boston. He was brought to Philadelphia, where he pleaded guilty to insurance fraud and was sentenced to two years in prison. But Geyer, convinced that he was also Pitezel's killer, persuaded the district attorney to indict him on another charge: homicide.

The Convict's Phlegm

The trial, which was held in front of a large audience, began on Monday, October 28, 1895, with the selection of the twelve members of the jury. It continued with the hearing of the witnesses and experts, and ended the following Saturday evening.

Holmes, in a stylish black suit, donning a mustache and beard, pleaded not guilty. A model prisoner, he chose to defend himself with what the *Chicago Daily Inter Ocean* called "the strangest narrative of the age."[11] During the trial, he suddenly changed his mind and asked to be defended by lawyers Samuel Rotan and William Shoemaker.[12] At the end of the pleas, the majority of the public as well as the lawyers were convinced that Holmes's would walk free as the prosecution was unable to prove his guilt in the Pitezel case. But the jurors were convinced of his guilt, and although they deliberated for two and a half hours, they did so "for the sake of appearances," having agreed in fact after less than a minute.[13] The verdict was returned at 8:45 p.m.: Holmes was convicted of first-degree murder.[14] During the trial he had not betrayed the slightest emotion, nor did he flinch when the judge read out the official document that confirmed his death by hanging.

The night before his execution on May 7, 1896— as every night during his imprisonment—Holmes was uncharacteristically stoic, carefully finishing his beef soup and picking up the crumbs of his bread before sipping his coffee and going to sleep around midnight. He was so fast asleep that guards struggled to wake him in the morning.

Sheriff Samuel W. Clement, leading Holmes to the gallows, was slightly apprehensive—this was his first execution. In accordance with official procedure, he was accompanied by his assistant, his deputy, and the prisoner's lawyer. Once he stood on the scaffold, which had been erected in the corridor between the cells, Holmes, whom the press later described as a man with "marvelous nerve,"[15] addressed the small audience in an unflinching voice and reaffirmed his partial innocence one final time:

> At 10:10 in the morning, he gave a calm speech: "Gentlemen, I have very few words to say. In fact, I would make no remarks at this time were it not that by not speaking I should acquiesce in my execution. I only wish to say that the extent of my wrong-doing in the taking of human life consists of contriving the killing of two women that have died at my hands as a result of criminal operations. I wish to state here, so there can be no chance of misunderstanding, that I am not guilty of taking the lives of any of the Pitezel family—the three children and Benjamin, the father, of whose death I was convicted, and for which I am today to be hanged. That is all I have to say."[16]

In an awkward gesture, he stepped up to his lawyer, shook his right hand and put his left hand on his shoulder. Finally, after buttoning his coat, he nodded to indicate that he was ready, offering a few reassuring words to the visibly nervous assistant superintendent Alexander Richardson: "Take your time, old man."[17] The sheriff proceeded with the protocol, tying his hands together and placing a black hood over his head, "and Holmes said, 'Good bye.' Other papers quoted his last conversation as the jailer asking 'Are you ready?' and Holmes responding with 'Yes; don't bungle; good-bye.' It was probably hard to make out what he was saying through the hood."[18]

At 10:02 a.m., the trap door opened; Holmes's body fell, his neck broke, his body jerking as it dangled in the air. His heart continued to beat for fifteen or twenty minutes.[19] His death was officially recorded thirty minutes later, at 10:32 a.m.[20]

Holmes's behavior during his detention has been dutifully recorded. Among other things, we know that he marked the days leading up to his execution on a calendar. Those around him, whether his guards, his lawyers, or the chaplain, all noted his calmness, claiming that they repeatedly saw him whistling in his cell. He also put together a library that included the Bible, Dr. Ewing's *Voice of Blood*, Homer, Virgil, religious books, Shakespeare's plays, a Latin grammar book, and a Greek dictionary. The doctors noted that he was in perfect health and had even gained weight while incarcerated.

In the days preceding the hanging, hammer blows resounded through the prison hall in the early morning as carpenters were building the gallows on the ground floor, in the wide corridor lined by the cells of those condemned to death. They worked for two days on end. When he was informed of the time of his execution, Holmes shaved the beard he had grown in jail, but kept his mustache. He asked for two favors: he wished to be given a lamp so that he could finish putting his papers in order during his last night, and he wanted his photographic portrait to be taken, which he planned to send to friends. Calm and focused, Holmes attended to his final arrangements, planning his burial down to the smallest detail. Among other things, he demanded to be buried in a place that should not be disclosed so as to prevent anyone from stealing his corpse for commercial purposes.

Prior to his execution, Holmes had been making headlines almost daily, as hardly anyone could remain indifferent to his crimes. His lawyer received the strangest of proposals, including offers to buy tickets for the execution (more than five hundred daily requests, with bids of up to $500). Business proposals poured in, one entrepreneur offering to cover the expenses of Holmes's burial in a bucolic spot in exchange for the right to collect an entrance fee to his tomb. Newspapers took part in the bidding as well, besieging Holmes for a scoop or exclusive rights to his confessions. One editor offered $1,000, only for his rival to raise the bid to $5,000, before a third one offered $7,500. From his prison cell, Holmes shrewdly negotiated his fees, and immediately after publishing a book in which he affirmed his innocence, proceeded to write several versions of a damning confession. In April 1896, his memoirs were printed simultaneously in three newspapers. The first version was published by the *Philadelphia Inquirer*, the second appeared simultaneously in the *Journal*, and the last, a seemingly more fictionalized version, in the *North American* (though its real authorship is in doubt). For this latter account, Holmes is said to have received upward of a staggering $7,500 from press magnate William Randolph Hearst. The money was destined for the education of his son, who was still living in Gilmanton with Holmes's first wife.

On the morning of his execution, the two ropes required by the protocol were duly recorded: one to be tied to the prisoner's neck, another in case there was a problem with the first.[21] The sheriff loosened the noose, but the rope had become so entangled that he struggled to free Holmes's body. After several unsuccessful attempts to turn the head of the condemned, he suggested to cut the rope, but Superintendent Perkins objected. After several long minutes of work, the deceased was finally pried loose. His face was ever so slightly discolored and deformed, his lips had turned black, his teeth were protruding, his eyes half open. The executioner recorded the presence of bruises and a burn on the neck on the spot where the rope had rubbed against the skin. Holmes's mortal remains were then carried away on a stretcher and put in a coffin that was placed in one of the crypts of Mount Moriah Cemetery, where it was scheduled to rest for two or three days. At Holmes's request, the lid of the casket was lifted, his body taken out, and mortar poured into the bottom before the body was placed back and covered in more cement. Holmes had requested this be done, as he wanted to make sure that his body would not be autopsied or stolen. That someone who killed dozens of people, cutting up and reassembling their bodies, should balk at the idea of his body being dissected after his death bears some irony.

Two days after the gallows had been erected, the thirty-five-year-old polygamous doctor, life-insurance scammer, dismemberer of corpses, inventor, and serial killer was dead, his body drowned in gallons of concrete.

[1] JD Crighton and Herman W. Mudgett, *Holmes' Own Story: Confessed 27 Murders; Lied then Died* [1895] (Murrieta, CA: Aerobear Classics, 1996), 11.

[2] Crighton and Mudgett, 11–12.

[3] Crighton and Mudgett.

[4] Erik Larson, *The Devil in the White City: Murder, Magic, and Madness at the Fair That Changed America* (New York: Bantam Books, 2004), 54.

[5] According to Adam Selzer, this story is an invention by Holmes: "Dr. Holton—usually said to be an old man killed by Holmes in later retellings of his story—was actually a young woman, Dr. Elizabeth Holton. [...] She died in 1933, having outlived Holmes by nearly four decades." Adam Selzer, *H. H. Holmes: The True History of the White City* (New York: Skyhorse, 2017), 597, Kindle.

[6] Holmes filed a suit to divorce his first wife shortly before, but the procedure eventually fell through.

[7] It was in his essay "The Tall Office Building Artistically Considered," published in March 1896 in *Lippincott's Monthly Magazine*, that the architect Louis Sullivan (1856–1924) coined one of the best-known axioms of modern architecture: "Form ever follows function. This is the law."

[8] Pulos, *American Design Ethic*, 180.

[9] Sigfried Giedion, *Space, Time and Architecture: The Growth of a New Tradition* (1941; Cambridge, MA: Harvard University Press, 2002), 10.

[10] For details on the investigation led by Frank Geyer, with the help of the Pinkerton detectives, and on how investigators discovered Holmes's scam and murders, see Frank Geyer, *The Holmes-Pitezel Case: A History of the Greatest Crime of the Century* (Philadelphia: Publisher's Union, 1896).

[11] Quoted in William Griffith, *The Trial of H. H. Holmes* (Chicago: Chicago Unbelievable, 2012), n.p.

[12] The *Philadelphia Inquirer* covered the whole process in detail.

[13] Griffith, *Trial of H. H. Holmes*, n.p.

[14] His lawyers unsuccessfully appealed.

[15] "H. H. Holmes Hanged His Marvelous Nerve with Him to the End on the Scaffold," *National Reflector*, May 9, 1896, 1.

[16] Crighton and Mudgett, *Holmes' Own Story*, 277.

[17] Adam Selzer, *The Curse of H. H. Holmes: The True Story of the Mysterious Tragedies* (Chicago: Chicago Unbelievable, 2012), n.p.

[18] Selzer.

[19] "Holmes Was Duly Hung," *Daily Olympian*, no. 48, May 8, 1896.

[20] "Murder Castle," *Chicago Sunday Tribune*, March 21, 1937, 77.

[21] Two dime-museum directors offered a large sum of money to buy the rope with which Holmes was hanged, but as required by law, Sheriff Clement handed it over to the prison archives.

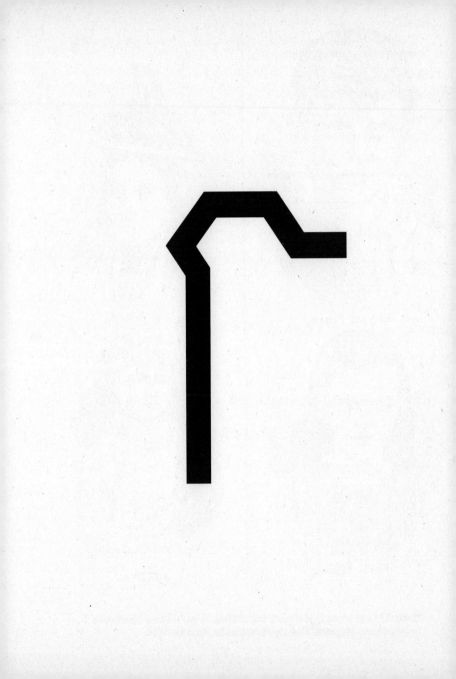

Howard Pitezel.

Mrs. Pitezel.

Nellie Pitezel.

Pearl Connor.

Illustrations of some of Holmes's first victims, from "Holmes Confesses Twenty-Seven Murders," *Philadelphia Inquirer*, April 12, 1896.

Minnie Williams.

Nannie Williams.

Mrs. Julia Connor.

Detective Geyer.

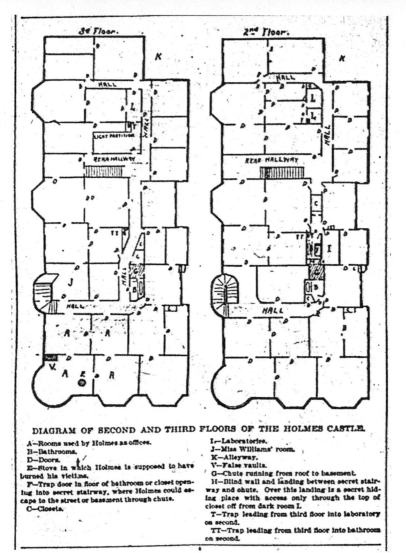

DIAGRAM OF SECOND AND THIRD FLOORS OF THE HOLMES CASTLE.

A—Rooms used by Holmes as offices.
B—Bathrooms.
D—Doors.
E—Stove in which Holmes is supposed to have burned his victims.
F—Trap door in floor of bathroom or closet opening into secret stairway, where Holmes could escape to the street or basement through chute.
C—Closets.

I.—Laboratories.
J—Miss Williams' room.
K—Alleyway.
V—False vaults.
G—Chute running from roof to basement.
H—Blind wall and landing between secret stairway and chute. Over this landing is a secret hiding place with access only through the top of closet off from dark room I.
T—Trap leading from third floor into laboratory on second.
TT—Trap leading from third floor into bathroom on second.

Technical drawing of two floors in Holmes's Castle, from "New Clews Found," *Chicago Times-Herald*, July 26, 1895.

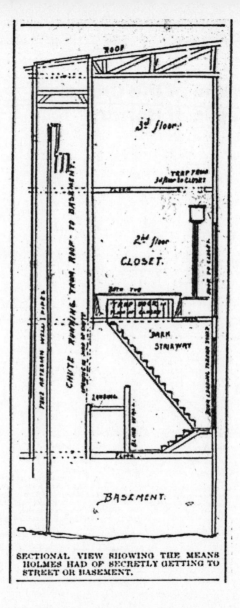

Sectional drawing showing Holmes's hidden access to his basement and the street, from "New Clews Found," *Chicago Times-Herald*, July 26, 1895.

3.

The Scene of the Crime:
The Castle of Horrors

Holmes was only able to commit his murders as easily as had he did because he built the house in which he operated. A killing machine with rooms, halls, and trapdoors designed with the sole intention of facilitating his crimes, the Castle was also a treasure trove of innovations. Besides a wall-to-wall gas and electricity supply system—at a time when most of his contemporaries were still lighting with candles—it included numerous modern contraptions, from asbestos-covered walls to a remote electric-control system and a huge furnace.

The Castle was an industrial site where "mechanization encounters the household," to borrow Giedion's language, which highlights the shared principles of household and factory management.[1] But Holmes's project is probably even closer to Catharine Beecher's conception according to which the house—beginning with its very layout—must be based on functional and rational organization.[2] In her bestselling *Treatise on Domestic Economy*, Beecher departs from rigid housing codes and traditional social relations in order to imagine an autonomous and independent model of society that values individuality.[3] This idea—albeit in a sense she could have hardly imagined— also lies at the heart of the individualism and inventiveness that characterize Holmes's practice.

Built of odds and ends (its complex layout unknown to the workers who built it), the Castle, with its three stories and basement, sat on a large lot of land of roughly 45 by 120 feet. Rare photographs of the building on 701–703 West 63rd Street show an edifice that towers over the surrounding buildings. The streets are lined with electric cables and service masts, bearing witness to the modernization of the neighborhood. The Castle's facades are punctuated by irregular semi-hexagonal bay windows, which have been rounded off. Striped fabric awnings protect the shop windows on the ground floor from the sun. The interior architecture was partly inspired by the reformist principles advocated by the British architect Charles Eastlake, who became known for a style in which "the lines were more resolutely rectilinear;

the interest in structural or seemingly structural ornament now erupted into a complicated, interlocked puzzle of parts, sometimes playful, sometimes awkward and bizarre."[4]

Beyond these references, few descriptions have survived, and those that remain are essentially related to Dr. Robinson's pharmacy on the ground floor, whose "interior, both ceiling and walls […] are decorated with frescoed stucco work which is delightfully arranged in mild colors. The floor is laid with alternating black and white diamond shaped tiling."[5] In its center stands "a massive pillar topped with an elaborate and elegant composite capital, radiant with harmonious colors, which supports a pen column of curved glass windows" topped with a cupola. The whole design "is arranged in such a manner as to dazzle the eyes of one who might attempt to study its pattern."[6]

In fact, the Castle blended Eastlake with Queen Anne Revival. The latter, popular during the 1870s, combined geometric patterns and simple shapes, a heterogeneous aesthetic that evoked "the fashionability of restraint" and sobriety.[7] The ground floor accommodated a row of businesses: a restaurant, a pharmacy, a jewelry store, a barber, a soap factory, Barton's Candy Store, and a small patent-filing office. The upper floors were reserved for office spaces and apartments for rent. Among the tenants were young stenographers—women—who came to work in the city and whom Holmes occasionally employed. A few months before the opening of the World's Fair in 1893, realizing that he could rent out additional rooms and small apartments to tourists, he added a second floor to the building, which he branded and advertised in the newspapers as "The World's Fair Hotel."

Hidden Vaults and Sealed Rooms, Graves and Crematories

What lay hidden inside Holmes's ostentatious building? It was later revealed that besides the shops, the Castle contained a series of rooms of various sizes; several narrow, labyrinthine passages; a removable wall at the end of a corridor; hidden staircases and trap doors; and even a secret room.

On the first floor, Holmes had set up his living quarters. The modest arrangement included a bedroom, a bathroom with a tub, and two adjacent rooms used as offices. Besides this private space, there were thirty-five rooms, six of which were bedrooms. Several rooms were windowless and airtight; in one of them stood a safe the size of which would have befitted a bank, connected with a pipe to the central gas system. The walls of one of the adjacent rooms were covered with sheets of iron and asbestos to prevent fire from spreading. Several trap doors hidden under carpets led from one floor to another—most notably in Holmes's bathroom, which gave him direct and discreet access to the basement, the drugstore's laboratory, the ground floor, and other rooms he deemed important.

Some rooms were soundproofed and others devised with ceilings so low that it was almost impossible to stand up in them; some were equipped with ladders that led to even smaller rooms located on others floors. The third, last-built story housed thirty-seven rooms, bedrooms, and furnished studios rented out to passing travelers and alcoholics wishing to cure their addiction (for which Holmes had found a remedy—or so his ads boasted).

The basement—the most secretive space—was the scene of Holmes's most sinister activities. Dug seven feet deep under the building, it was divided into several independent sections, some of which were connected to the upper floors of the house by a secret staircase and a dumbwaiter. A crematory was built into the wall,[8] and under the brick vaults a series of steps led to a torch-lit subbasement where two six-feet-long, three-feet-wide tanks full of quicklime and acid gave off a nauseating smell. Under another vault, Holmes had commissioned a carpenter to construct a fifty-by-twenty-inch sealed pinewood box whose interior was covered with tar. Fitted with handles, it could be used to transport the trunks of his victims. Finally, in a corner under the chute departing from Holmes's private apartment stood a dissecting table complete with surgical instruments and the infamously large furnace.

A Climatology of Murder:
The Original "Smart House"

Until around 1880, the majority of homes in the United States were lit by oil lamps and candles. These were either homemade or, more rarely, purchased in stores. The arrival of domestic gas raised a problem of energetic household autonomy: city dwellers, whose habits were well entrenched, were hesitant at first. They were frightened of gas because of the disasters it could cause—not least because it would be quickly adopted as a means for suicide. In the fractious history of the relationships between technology and health, gas—an invisible and odorless substance—was long considered a silent threat. Terrifying accounts abounded in the press. A deadly and invasive medium, gas spreads invisibly, disrupting the comfort of the home by affecting "not only the olfactory nerves, but the pulmonary organs."[9] Moreover, households were wary of losing their autonomy: "Once a house was connected to a central gas supply, its autonomy was over. [...] With a public gas supply, domestic lighting entered its industrial—and dependent—stage. No longer self-sufficiently producing its own heat and light, each house was inextricably linked to an industrial energy producer. This loss of domestic autonomy is part of the larger dissolution of the 'total household.'"[10] These concerns were hotly debated, with many reluctant to outfit their homes accordingly. Gas companies, in turn, had not anticipated that citizens would fight to maintain their independence from a grid they did not control. As the home became a cog in a larger system, it literally opened itself up to the machinic invasion. The impurity of gas was illustrated by the sprawling metaphor of the cephalopod: "To contemporaries it seemed that industries were expanding, sending out tentacles, octopus-like, into every home. Being connected to them as consumers made people uneasy. They clearly felt a loss of personal freedom."[11] For all these reasons, up until the 1880s, the majority of homes in large cities in the United States still used Argand lamps, which ran on expensive whale oil.

Holmes did not share these concerns. On the contrary, he was quick to connect his house to the area's first gas and electricity grid. Panels in his apartment, which were connected to electric sensors hidden behind wooden slats, enabled him to register the comings and goings of the Castle's occupants. An electric bell sounded each time the main door to his floor was opened, and a gauge allowed him to monitor the movements of his employees and future victims without having to expose himself or leave his private quarters.

The spread of industrialized machines, the expansion of factories, and thus a factory-based workforce, and the emergence of a broad middle class at the end of the nineteenth century must be seen in light of the rise of productivity as the new ideal, with cities the main sites of these transformations. The gap between the modern way of life and a traditional sensibility gave birth to a new relationship to dwelling.[12] City residents of that time aspired to a form of urban retreat embellished with a "decorative landscape," in the words of the French historian and art critic Alphonse Germain, who as early as 1891 described the externalization of feelings in decorative art.[13] Germain emphasized the transformative power of the decorative landscape by imagining a model of pastoral interior symbolized by an "oasis of greenery" that would shape the spirit and soul of its inhabitants while evoking an idealized refuge.[14] The French journals *Art et décoration* and *L'Art décoratif* further developed his concept by pairing it with the "psychology of the rooms," that is, recommending certain colors and forms conducive to the production of a certain environment in "a wonderfully domestic variant on the modernist expressive self-sufficiency of pictorial elements. The desired goal, simply stated, was the creation of a pastoral realm for physical and mental reflection in which the decor contributed to, rather than detracted from, the refreshing of the weary brain-worker."[15] While the home-as-shelter long constituted an ideal "home sweet home," a refuge available only to the affluent, the very concept runs counter to Holmes's functionalist ideal.

Pushing standardization to its limits, Holmes designed his home as a tool for suffering and torment. Combining murder with mechanization, he harnessed rationalization to satisfy his grizzly desires. Instead of speculating on the stock market, he lived off the return on investment from his household furnishings—first and foremost gas and electricity on all floors: "I confined him within the secret room and slowly starved him to death. Of this room and its secret gas supply and muffled windows and doors, sufficient has already been printed," he writes in the first of his confessions.[16]

Gas had yet another advantage: it allowed him to kill at a remote distance. From his room, he could let the gas spread into a specially furnished room at the other end of the Castle. Then, by setting off a spark—still without moving from his apartment—he could transform that room into a furnace, its asbestos-covered walls containing the fire. He even went so far as to fit the room with shut-off valves in plain sight, deceiving his victims into believing they could stop the deadly influx of gas. But while the valves were fake, their function was not merely decorative, as they accelerated the victims' nervous exhaustion, and hence their willingness to relinquish their earthly possessions—life insurance policies, shares, real estate, etc.—to Holmes, who was meanwhile sitting comfortably in his apartment.[17]

Holmes's Castle comprised an impressive list of technological innovations, from boilers, gas tanks, and pipes between bathrooms to a dedicated wastewater drainage system.[18] Architects of the time recommended installing the bathroom on the second floor of the house, "near the attic tank or cistern, the most common source of indoor water, and close to the bedrooms, where personal washing was traditionally done."[19] In *The Architecture of Country Houses of 1850*, A. J. Downing urged his colleagues to promote the use of bathrooms by adjoining them to bedrooms.[20] Did Holmes follow Downing's advice when he installed his bathroom next to his bedroom? We may only speculate if he read Downing, but as he was by no means a fainthearted bourgeois for whom "such a home was still a fantasy,"[21] we can easily imagine that, galvanized by the numerous treaties on household economy published in his time, he was convinced of the benefits of modern technologies.

Holmes was ahead of his time. He was well informed on the latest technology and the newest trends in interior design and decoration. This is not least evidenced by the presence of a dumbwaiter in his home. A rare appliance at the time, this type of elevator had been invented to facilitate the work of domestic servants in multistory houses. In 1841, Beecher praised the benefits of this "convenience which saves much labor."[22] Ten years later, phrenologist Orson S. Fowler, marveling at the invention, celebrated this "contrivance worth $100 to any $1,000 house."[23] For Holmes, however, it was not intended to facilitate the transport of food from one floor to another: his modern palace was equipped with a dumbwaiter "large enough to accommodate a body."[24] Yet Holmes did not so much reinterpret the functionality of this and other devices as use them in the way their inventors might have indicated in the user instructions: "A large dumb-waiter connected with the basement, as did two greased chutes, one from the second floor and the other from the third. Holmes [...] could murder in the building at any point he found convenient and sent the body of his victim zipping down below with the utmost dispatch."[25]

But what of the large furnace, originally presented to Holmes by an inventor hoping to patent it, and its relation to design? It was comprised of an inner chamber built of firebrick and required regular and careful maintenance to ensure the burner reached the desired temperature. Its sheer size raised eyebrows and prompted the wildest speculations, until Holmes clarified its use in his confessions. It had been devised by a man named Warner to enable the production of glass plates the size of a man. Although Holmes subsequently made only minor changes to the original design, he always claimed to be its actual inventor. Underneath the furnace, he added steel rails on which he could roll a cart; above it, he built an arch with a peephole that, according to his initial testimony, allowed him to observe the inside of the oven and check the temperatures to make sure the glass curved without melting. Investigators reached an entirely different conclusion: they believe that the oven allowed him to dispose of his victims' bodies, the peephole allowed him to check the state of calcination of the bodies, and the cart was used to move the corpses around from one end of the oven chamber to the other. The flue gas escaped through a ventilation duct in the small brick chamber, making it possible for the bodies to disappear without any inconvenient smells invading the Castle. Holmes found its use so satisfactory that when the furnace was destroyed in a fire, he decided to build another one: "Holmes would be one of the first to realize the infallibility of a cremator as a destroyer of evidence of his guilt."[26]

60

All these contraptions helped Holmes to increase productivity. Not content with making his victims work for him and dispossessing them of their savings before disposing of them, he even made a profit from their corporeal remains. In his torch-lit basement laboratory he dismembered their corpses on dissecting tables. The flesh was dissolved in vats filled with quicklime in a room next door, the bones reassembled into skeletons, which he then sold to medical institutions through an unnamed middleman: "To him I sold this man's body as well as others at later dates; in short, in this writing, in each instance, when the manner of the disposal of their remains is not otherwise specified, it will be understood that they are turned over to him, he paying me from $25 to $45 for each body."[27] As they inspected the Castle as part of their investigation, the Pinkerton detectives found receipts for these transactions. Perusing the newspapers, they also discovered a small ad posted by Holmes looking for a qualified employee:

> WANTED. Skeleton articulator. Apply H. H. Holmes. 701 Sixty-Third Street. After noon.[28]

Published two years before the first women disappeared in the Castle, the ad was answered by M. G. Chappell, who was put to work. When questioned by the police, Chappell later explained that Holmes enjoyed watching him cut up the bodies and soon offered to assist him. He also remembered that the first skeleton on which he had worked was that of a woman; presented with a photograph, he recognized Emeline Cigrand, Holmes's young mistress from Nebraska. After Chappell's expert treatment, her skeleton entered the anatomy class at Hahnemann Medical College.[29]

During their search, detectives also found bones in the rooms of the real estate office Holmes had established on the second floor. Holmes insisted they were beef bones from the time the premises had accommodated a restaurant during the World's Fair, which was also the reason for the installation of a dumbwaiter. But "there were bones virtually all over the structure"[30]; as well as a gold watch, teeth, and metal parts of shoes belonging to Julia Connor; the Williams sisters' jewelry; and a small intact skeleton, probably Conner's baby—all casting further doubts on Holmes's account. When walking past a windowless bathroom, detectives noticed that the flame of their candle started to flicker and lean to one side, pointing to the presence of a hidden air duct. The discovery of a secret space behind the fake wall eventually led them to the part of the basement where Holmes had handled the corpses.

Taking a closer look at the section and elevation plans of his house, they then unraveled a maze of secret corridors, passageways, staircases, and sliding walls, from which they concluded that Holmes could effectively move around the house without being noticed. A hatch in the bathroom enabled him to access the floor below; behind one of the two doors in his room lay a staircase that led outside, while the other door opened onto a chute that ran to the center of the basement. Holmes's movements, it turned out, were by no means as restricted as his guests'. Once they had died, they became mobile again thanks to the dumbwaiter and other furnishings in the house. Their bodies traveled over hidden routes until reaching the cellar, where they were buried, burned, or decomposed.

In his initial confessions, Holmes detailed the method with which he killed each of his victims: Lizzie, a servant, was the first victim to suffocate in the vault of the basement; Robert Latimer, the first janitor of the Castle, was locked into one of the secret rooms, where he was starved to death; and Warner, from the Warner Glass Bending company, died in the furnace of his own invention.

Thanks to the receipts discovered during the investigation, there is some idea of the extent of Holmes's skeleton business: that of an old friend, for example, was sold to an acquaintance at the University of Chicago.
The only murders that were not perpetrated in the Castle were those of Benjamin Pitezel and his children.

In 1893 and 1895, several fires—presumably commissioned by Holmes in order to collect the insurance money and get rid of compromising evidence—ripped through the Castle. In the meantime, journalists and investigators were able to visit and inspect the building. They took notes and made drawings that are valuable documents for understanding the complex. The purposeful design of the Castle was so important to Holmes that in 1894, after the end of the World's Fair, he considered rebuilding it (under the name of O. C. Pratt) elsewhere, in Fort Worth, Texas, on land that belonged to the Williams sisters. On July 28, 1895, as his trial was making front-page news, five thousand people queued in front of the Castle for a visit, with jeweler E. C. Davis charging a ten-cent entrance fee. Having been partly destroyed by the first fire, an application for reconstruction was filed with City Hall on August 9, 1895. But a new explosion rocked the Castle on August 18, hollowing out the building and destroying the remaining evidence of Holmes's crimes. On August 27, the two upper floors were taken down for security reasons, to be rebuilt and accommodate new tenants. The cause of the explosions—arson or a gas leak due to the general state of disrepair—remains unknown. More fire broke out in 1903, and again in 1915. In January 1938, the Federal State purchased the property from one Emma Morrison for $61,000. Today, nothing is left of it, the lot on which it stood now home to a post office and a parking garage, both built in May 1938.

Scams and Murders on All Floors

The Castle obeyed the logic of mass production—of life and death alike. Holmes was a businessman who conducted his activities with the aim of turning a profit. All in all, he employed more than five hundred workmen in the construction of his building, who were routinely fired as quickly as they had been hired. Keeping up an unusually high turnover served a double purpose, as it ensured that none of the workers could ever guess the actual functions of the various rooms, while also as a pretext for withholding payment of their fees.

In addition, the construction materials for the Castle were generally bought on credit. By refusing to pay his debts (he was sued by the most obstinate of his many creditors, some of whom he did not hesitate to intimidate), Holmes was able to keep his expenses down. When a company proceeded to repossess a large safe that he had bought on credit and fitted into one of the rooms, he threatened to sue them, arguing that it could not be removed without endangering the structural integrity of the building. Faced with this and similar threats, most creditors preferred to cut their losses.

Once the Castle was up and running, Holmes expanded his scamming repertoire. Among others, most items on sale in his street-level drugstore were fake. The in-store jewelry counter sold colored glass beads of various sizes, and regardless of their prescription, customers consistently walked out of the store with the same scented chalk powder. Holmes also sold medicinal cures, notably against alcoholism, as well as a magic potion that customers could source directly from a fountain in the pharmacy or buy in bottles. During their investigation, detectives discovered a hidden barrel in the basement that was connected to the water mains through a pipe leading straight up to the fountain: the miraculous potion turned out to be ordinary tap water infused with herbs—also known as the famed Linden Grove Mineral Water.

When Holmes was first investigated, the police did not suspect he was a violent criminal, let alone a serial killer. He was initially pursued for fraud and sentenced to two years' imprisonment. Although detectives knew of the existence of secret rooms in the Castle, they failed to work out their true purpose. For want of a better explanation, they were thought to be storage spaces where Holmes hid unpaid items from the Tobey Furniture Company and mattresses "belonging to Schultz and Hirsh [sic] of Van Buren and Des Plaines streets."[31] His secret cache was worth thousands of dollars.

Holmes also thought up an elaborate scam involving the city's gas mains. Ever the operator, he established business relations with Canadian investors who eventually traveled to Chicago hoping to buying his patent for domestic gas production. Sided by a chemist, Holmes introduced himself to his foreign clients as the inventor of the Chemical-Water Gas Generator, a machine capable of transforming ordinary tap water into gaseous fuel. To this end, he had built a complex contraption of pipes, ducts, and vats in the basement of the Castle, which the Canadian experts agreed to buy for $10,000. Back home, they attempted to replicate the experience, but to no avail—unsurprisingly so, as Holmes had merely connected his "invention" to the public gas supply via a hidden pipe. He was eventually found out, but the gas company decided not to press charges.

At the end of the nineteenth century—that is, decades before theories of so-called public communication examined how the masses could be manipulated through advertising[32]— the phenomenon was already long in the making. Never one to be outdone, Holmes actively advertised the drugs, paint, and ointments available in his drugstore, as well as his magic potion, which, according to various accounts, was sold for $5 and $10 a glass, or $25 a bottle. Like a modern-day magician, he used advertising to sell everything and anything, including the reassembled skeletons from his basement.

Economy, Productivity, and the Modern Body

According to Marx's luminous observation, "A philosopher produces ideas, a poet poems, a clergyman sermons, a professor compendia and so on. A criminal produces crimes. If we look a little closer at the connection between this latter branch of production and society as a whole, we shall rid ourselves of many prejudices."[33] Like an obsessional machine, Holmes's Castle was instrumental in the transformation of bodies, whether they disappeared in a furnace or in quicklime vats, or came back to life as skeletons. The same holds true for his numerous scams, from peddling a cure against alcohol addiction to selling water from the fountain of eternal youth. In the various rooms of the Castle, Holmes strove to transform the human body, whether through the promise of eternal rejuvenation or, more frequently, eternal rest. The most appalling byproduct of this transformation was no doubt the income he generated from the corpses, a process that can be likened to the modern idea of obsolescence as a kind of "creative waste," as theorized by Christine Frederick in the 1920s. "It is now time to assert," writes the theoretician of domestic economy, "*the policy of creative waste in spending.*"[34] By stating "the housewife's moral obligation to rhythmically buy and discard products [Frederick] elevated the garbage of consumer culture into a form of positive production, valuing the destruction and replacement of objects as a pleasurable and socially instrumental act. Frederick and other promoters of consumerism conceived of 'waste' not merely as an incidental by-product, a final residue, of the consumption cycle, but as a generative, necessary force."[35]

Holmes's practice evidences the same dynamic, fleeting forces of creative loss that Frederick had in mind when she wrote: "There isn't the slightest reason in the world why materials which are inexhaustibly replenishable should not be creatively 'wasted.'"[36] Creative waste forms an integral part of an economy subjected to a constant cycle of consumption and resupply of consumer goods. This logic also underpinned the Castle, where everything was designed to boost Holmes's earnings. Could we then say that he is, to a certain extent, the incarnation of the perfect American citizen at the start of the twentieth century, someone who embodied the rise of capitalism in his country? Surely, Marx's ironic praise of the crime economy would tend to corroborate this view: "The criminal breaks the monotony and everyday security of bourgeois life. In this way he keeps it from stagnation, and gives rise to that uneasy tension and agility without which even the spur of competition would get blunted. Thus he gives a stimulus to the productive forces."[37] After all, is it not true that, "[t]orture alone has given rise to the most ingenious mechanical inventions, and employed many honorable craftsmen in the production of its instruments?"[38] Beyond its productive and inventive dimension, crime ultimately contributes to regulating the workforce and keeping wages high: "While crime takes a part of the superfluous population off the labor market and thus reduces competition among the laborers—up to a certain point preventing wages from falling below the minimum—the struggle against crime absorbs another part of this population. Thus the criminal comes in as one of those natural 'counterweights' which bring about a correct balance and open up a whole perspective of 'useful' occupations."[39]

The remote operation of the Castle's technological devices—the dumbwaiter, the electrical circuit, the Warner furnace, etc.—suggests a relationship of equivalence between domestic space and economy, a rapport that the serial nature of Holmes's murders echoes; that is, the fluidity and multiple forms that characterize energy and capitalistic financial transactions alike. This is best illustrated by the functionality of the gas grid, a metaphor for the disembodied circulation of capital. Whether we look at them from the standpoint of "creative waste" or the immateriality of financial transactions, Holmes's murders—committed in order to increase his prosperity by converting the dead into money—bear witness to a sound understanding of economic principles. Holmes was sensitive to the methods of mass consumption and the techniques of modern advertising, and his Castle was a model of economy—harking back to the Greek etymology of the word, which denotes the "management of the household."[40] The production of Holmes's wealth and the production of his crimes are but two manifestations of the same postulate.

[1] Giedion, *Mechanization Takes Command*, 512. For Giedion, however, the "factory and the household have only one factor in common, but a crucial one. Both must improve organization and curtail waste labor. This is the goal to which the whole development tends."

[2] See Catharine Beecher, "On the Construction of Houses," in *Treatise on Domestic Economy* [1841], https://www.gutenberg.org /files/21829/21829-h/21829-h.htm.

[3] "The most important characteristic of this new domestic space was its ability to integrate personal and national goals. It fostered uniform communities, molded socially homogeneous human beings, and produced a set of predictable habits among contemporary Americans. To do this and at the same time defend the virtues of self-reliance, freedom of choice, and independence of mind required considerable ingenuity. Catharine Beecher was among the first to engage in the contradictory task of both nationalizing and personalizing the American domestic environment." Kathryn Kish Sklar, *Catharine Beecher: A Study in American Domesticity* (New York: Norton Press, 1981), xii.

[4] Gwendolyn Wright, *Building the Dream: A Social History of Housing in America* (Cambridge, MA: MIT Press, 1983), 61.

[5] Robert L. Corbitt, *The Holmes Castle: The Only True Account of the Greatest Criminal the Police Have Ever Handled* (Chicago: Corbitt and Morrison, 1895), 14–15.

[6] Corbitt, 14.

[7] Wright, *Building the Dream*, 241.

[8] The first modern crematory was built in 1876 in Washington, Pennsylvania, by doctor Francis Julius LeMoyne. It was used for the first voluntary cremation on December 6 of the same year. See Margaret C. McCulloch, *Fearless Advocate of the Right: The Life of Francis J. LeMoyne, M.D., 1798–1879* (Boston: Christopher Publishing House, 1941).

[9] Andrew J. Downing, *Architecture of Country Houses* (1850; New York: Dover Publications, 1969), 475.

[10] Wolfgang Schivelbusch, *Disenchanted Night: The Industrialization of Light in the Nineteenth Century*, trans. Angela Davies (Berkeley: University of California Press, 1988), 28.

[11] Schivelbusch, 29.

[12] See Georg Simmel, "The Metropolis and Mental Life" (1903) in *The Sociology of Georg Simmel*, ed. and trans. K. H. Wolff (New York: Free Press, 1950), 409–24. Simmel describes this neurosis as a consequence of life in the metropolis.

[13] Alphonse Germain, "Le paysage décoratif," *L'Ermitage* 2 (November 1891), 641–45; my translation.

[14] Joyce Henri Robinson, "'Hi Honey, I'm Home': Weary (Neurasthenic) Businessmen and the Formation of a Serenely Modern Aesthetic," in *What Is Architecture?*, ed. Andrew Ballantyne (London: Routledge, 2002), 129.

[15] Robinson, "'Hi Honey,'" 117.

[16] "Confession of H. H. Holmes," 345.

[17] See Herbert Asbury, *Gem of the Prairie: An Informal History of the Chicago Underworld* (New York: Knopf, 1940), 183.

[18] Although still expensive around 1880, hot-air and hot-water boilers in the basement, connected to a maze of pipes and meters, slowly made their way into middle-class homes, where wood-fired ovens were still the norm.

[19] Merritt Ierley, *The Comforts of Home: The American House and the Evolution of Modern Convenience* (New York: Clarkson Potter, 1999), 99.

[20] Downing, *Architecture of Country Houses*, 308.

[21] Ierley, *Comforts of Home*, 13.

[22] "By this method, almost every thing needed to pass between the kitchen and parlor can be sent up and down, without any steps." Beecher, "On the Construction of Houses," 278–79.

[23] Orson S. Fowler, *A Home for All, Or, the Gravel Wall and Octagon Mode of Building* (New York: Fowlers and Wells, 1853), 122.

[24] David Franke, *The Torture Doctor* (New York: Hawthorne, 1975), 89.

[25] Charles Boswell and Lewis Thompson, *The Girls in Nightmare House* (New York: Fawcett Publications, 1955), 91.

[26] "Eyewitness Account: Anonymous Furnace Maker," *Chicago Daily Inter Ocean*, July 24, 1895, quoted in William Griffith and Adam Selzer, *The Murder Castle of H. H. Holmes: A Scrapbook of Eyewitness Accounts, Diagrams, and Ephemera* (Chicago: Chicago Unbelievable, 2012), n.p.

[27] Crighton and Mudgett, *Holmes' Own Story*, 288.

[28] Alan Hynd, "Blubeard and the Missing Twenty," (unpublished manuscript, July 31, 1940) Pinkerton Private Detective Archives, Manuscript Department, Library of Congress, Washington, DC.

[29] See Adam Selzer, "H. H. Holmes and Mr. Chappell, the Skeleton Articulator," *Mysterious Chicago*, October 4, 2013, http://mysteriouschicago.com/hh-holmes-and-mr-chappell-the-skeleton-articulator.

[30] Hynd, "Blubeard and the Missing Twenty."

[31] "Hid in Secret Rooms," *Chicago Daily Tribune*, March 31, 1893, https://www.newspapers.com/clip/19481262/chicago-tribune/.

[32] See Edward L. Bernays, *Propaganda: The Public Mind in the Making* (New York: Horace Liveright, 1928).

33 Marx, "Apologist Conception of the Productivity of All Professions," 948.

34 Christine Frederick, *Selling Mrs. Consumer* (New York: Business Bourse, 1929), 79.

35 Ellen Lupton and J. Abbott Miller, *The Bathroom, the Kitchen, and the Aesthetics of Waste: A Process of Elimination* (New York: Kiosk, 1992), 7. The authors go on to state that "in the consumer economy, 'production' finds a place *inside* the process of consumption, a cycle that reiterates the body's own form of 'creative waste,' excrement."

36 Frederick, *Selling Mrs. Consumer*, 252–53.

37 Marx, "Apologist Conception of the Productivity of All Professions," 950.

38 Marx, 949.

39 Marx, 950.

40 *Oikonomia*, from *oikos*, "house," and *nemein*, "to manage."

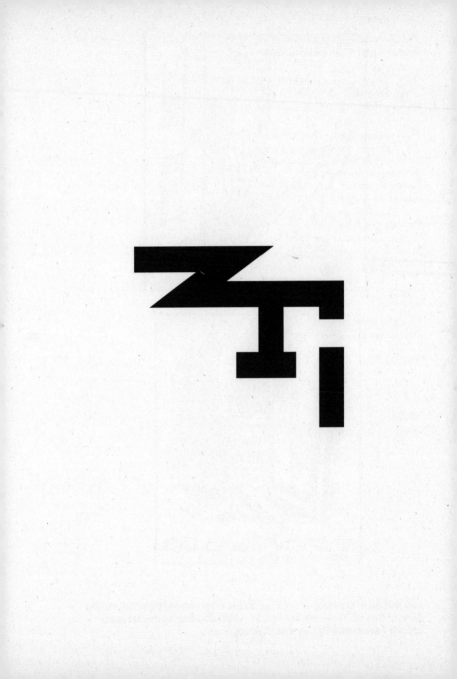

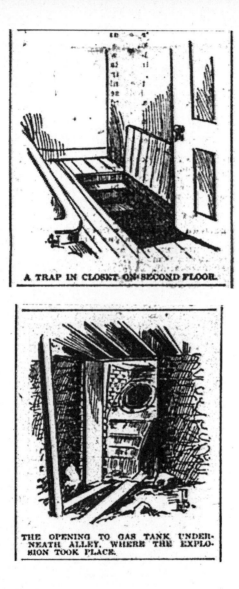

A TRAP IN CLOSET ON SECOND FLOOR.

THE OPENING TO GAS TANK UNDER-
NEATH ALLEY, WHERE THE EXPLO-
SION TOOK PLACE.

Left and right: Newspaper sketches of the crime scene, from "Ribs in the
Ashes," *Sunday Times-Herald*, July 21, 1895. Courtesy of the Abraham
Lincoln Presidential Library and Museum.

HOLMES' PRIVATE LABORATORY.

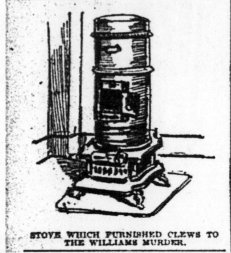

STOVE WHICH FURNISHED CLEWS TO
THE WILLIAMS MURDER.

THE SEARCHERS.
WORKING BY ELECTRIC LIGHT

Left and right: Newspaper sketch of police searching the crime scene, from "Bad Slip of Holmes," *Chicago Daily Tribune*, July 25, 1895. Courtesy of the Abraham Lincoln Presidential Library and Museum.

WHERE THE BONES WERE FOUND

4.

The Scars of Evil

What to make of Holmes's final con job? While in prison awaiting trial, Holmes alleged that his body was undergoing inexplicable physical changes. In his first confession—written for posterity but, in the much shorter term, the avid readers of the *Philadelphia Inquirer*—he claimed to be possessed by the devil: "My features are assuming a pronounced satanical cast. I have become afflicted with that dread disease, rare but terrible, with which physicians are acquainted, but over which they have no control whatsoever. That disease is a malformation or distortion of the osseous parts… My head and face are gradually assuming an elongated shape. I believe fully that I am growing to resemble the devil—that the similitude is almost completed."[1] The astonishing transmutation was supposed to "explain" his crimes, with Holmes presenting himself as a victim of a modern illness.

The pathological "distortion" invoked by Holmes can be traced back to a concept introduced by the French psychiatrist Bénédict Morel in his 1857 book *Traité des dégénérescences physiques, intellectuelles et morales de l'espèce humaine et des causes qui produisent ces variétés maladives* (Treatise on physical, intellectual, and moral degenerations of the human species and the causes that produce these sickly variations). Supporting Holmes's claim, the portrait accompanying his confession shows him donning a goatee and a kind of toque. He no longer looks the irresistible, charismatic seducer of past photographs but seems to have metamorphosed. Holmes appears to have worried about his condition, wondering aloud if his body reflected his damned soul: "Today I have every attribute of a degenerate—a moral idiot. Is it possible that the crimes, instead of being the result of these abnormal conditions, are in themselves the occasion of the degeneracy?"[2] We may legitimately ask ourselves if Holmes had read Oscar Wilde's scandalous 1890 novel *The Picture of Dorian Gray*, from which might have been borrowed the idea that the body can conceal or expose the stigmata of the soul's crimes and lies, or the immorality of the philanderer and murderer. Wilde's character pursues a hedonistic lifestyle, all the while observing the progressive deformation of his painted portrait as it records his sins; his duplicitous nature only manifests in the final moment when he stabs the canvas. In Wilde's story, the evidence of Gray's damned soul does not entirely disappear; it is merely confined within the work of art. By negating the rationality of his actions and presenting himself as the victim of an imaginary disease, Holmes tried to recast himself as a wretched soul.

The Dark Side of Design

In *Mechanization Takes Command*, Giedion affirms that he wants to encourage readers to rethink the relationships between humans and automation. To this effect, he attempts to retrace the metamorphosis of the US landscape at the end of the nineteenth century against the backdrop of technological developments. By this, he essentially means that anonymous achievements and objects are the last bastion of humankind, whose "activities [to the people of the nineteenth century] seemed unimportant and without significance, either good or bad."[3]

      Giedion then dwells on the invention of the assembly line and its various modifications and improvements since Oliver Evans, the late eighteenth-century inventor. Among others, he focuses on British spinning factories, where the alignment of machines was perfected between 1850 and 1890. He goes on to retrace how the modern assembly line was established in Cincinnati and Chicago from 1865, before it was automatized around 1920, asking: "Would it not be possible to mechanize meat production too? Enterprising and inventive people tried their hand at this problem. Efforts were made to develop machines for almost every one of the time-consuming operations. Yet […] a complex organic substance with its contingencies, its changing, easily vulnerable structure, is something other than a piece of amorphous iron. [...] This was true also of a dead animal. Despite many attempts, processing of its carcass could not be fully mechanized."[4] Nevertheless, as soon as "mass production was used to turn the live animal into salable meat, sharp and thorough division into single operations became necessary, as in all mechanization."[5]

Giedion then zooms in on Chicago to describe the cutting-up techniques in the city's slaughterhouses, where the culling quota for cattle reached 60,000 head a day in 1871. The establishment of Union Stock Yards, covering an area of more than 150 hectares, transformed Chicago into the country's biggest trading center for livestock, where thousands and soon millions of animals were processed. They were slaughtered, butchered, and transformed on site into meat, soups, glues, soaps, fertilizers, and much more. "They use everything about the hog except the squeal," says one character in *The Jungle*.[6]

The city's slaughterhouses introduced ever-new standardization techniques to increase the culling rates for chickens, pigs, cattle, and lambs; animals transited through the abattoirs as objects.[7] To explain their mode of operation, Giedion looks at the industrial treatment of hogs, underlining the complexity of slaughtering and processing. Ultimately, the omnivore that served as a model for the development of the modern assembly line turned out to be lacking in efficiency, for "in the slaughtering process the material to be handled is a complex, irregularly shaped object: the hog. Even when dead, the hog largely refuses to submit to the machine."[8]

The objectification of the living results from the merger of efficiency and mechanization that characterizes the industrial revolution. It spares no animal—nonhuman or human. The hog and its fellow animals are but commodities subjected to the laws of profit. Despite protestations to the contrary in the introduction and conclusion of his treatise, the pages that Giedion devotes to this question in the context of US slaughterhouses at the end of the nineteenth century point to unresolved ambiguities concerning the status and standardization of life once functionalism had been declared the moral blueprint of industrial activity. This perspective is further complicated by the working conditions endured by factory workers who were struggling to keep up with the workload and the pace of the assembly line. In many cases, they were forbidden to wear watches in order to prevent them from monitoring their schedules themselves and dissociating their working hours from their rest time.[9]

Giedion's examination of the consequences of standardization was published in 1948, that is, three years after the end of World War II. The postwar context led him to revise his position, putting his initial enthusiasm into perspective and expressing his concerns about the themes he had developed in his earlier work by pointing out that mechanization neutralizes our sensitivity to death:

> What is truly startling in this mass transition from life to death is the complete neutrality of the act. One does not experience, one does not feel; one merely observes. It may be that nerves that we do not control rebel somewhere in the subconscious. Days later, the inhaled odor of blood suddenly rises from the walls of one's stomach, although no trace of it can have clung to the person. How far the question is justified we do not know, nevertheless it may be asked: has this neutrality toward death had any further effect upon us? This broader influence does not have to appear in the land that evolved mechanized killing, or even at the time the methods came about.[10]

In trying to explain this loss of sensitivity in the face of standardized slaughter, Giedion takes a significant sidestep, evoking the technical descriptions of slaughtering in his book to examine the implications of this technical revolution and the way it changed our way of thinking: "This neutrality toward death may be lodged deep in the roots of our time. It did not bare itself on a large scale until the War, when whole populations, as defenseless as the animals hooked head downwards on the traveling chain, were obliterated with trained neutrality."[11] In other words, he questions the relationship between the standardization of death applied to animals and the industrial organization underpinning the "manufacturing of corpses" in Nazi concentration camps.

Contemporary commentators on Holmes's trial already framed his "crime factory" in both the local context of Chicago's "mechanized death phenomenon" and the wider context of the demise of the metropolis. As one journalist put it, Holmes's story tended to "illustrate the end of the century"[12]—a fin de siècle overshadowed by the industrial revolution. Several decades later, Mark Seltzer expands on this idea: "The apparatuses of mass slaughter and mechanized organic disassembly lines constitute what Sigfried Giedion describes as the development of an elaborate 'murder machinery' and the 'mechanization of death.'"[13] It is under this angle that Holmes's activity as a "serial killer" commends further examination. Fascinated by the combination of murder and industry, Holmes saw technique as the most effective way to attain his objectives.

The serial nature of his murders exposes the horror inherent in the principles of rationality and the ergonomics presiding over them, while also showing how the murderer's violence echoes the innate violence of standardization. Holmes's practice can therefore be seen as a sort of aftershock, in the seismic sense of the term, of industrialization imposed on the living.

This, then, is the nightmarish and violent expression of a design that clearly exceeds the canonical moral definition of the discipline posited by its founders—unless, that is, we follow Flusser's analysis: "The word *design* has come to occupy the position it has in contemporary discourse through our awareness that being a human being is a design against nature. […] The word design has managed to retain its key position in everyday discourse because we are starting (perhaps rightly) to lose faith in art and technology as sources of value."[14]

The Art of Design

We may ask ourselves if the principle of a "zone of silence," through which Banham set out to explore the obvious omissions in the narrative of modern architecture, could not be transposed and applied to the history of design. Any such questioning of the conventions of the discipline and its definition is aimed at deconstructing the original misunderstanding of design as an expression of virtue. In this sense, the figure of H. H. Holmes fills one of the gaps in the history of industry. As Wilson has suggested, his practice bears similarities to that of the great industrialist Henry Ford. To accept this view, which puts serial killers on a par with the great inventors and entrepreneurs who revolutionized the United States, also means to consider them as heirs of the anonymous engineer portrayed by Giedion.

By interrogating and rethinking the models of design history, their modern axis is disrupted. Their grand narratives are based on celebrations of a virtuous myth presented as two opposite poles: Pevsner's "pioneer" or "hero" narrative versus Giedion's general perspective, which dispenses with individual signature styles. However, beyond their oppositions, these two views converge when it comes to defining the moral role of the designer in charge of the industrial production of "good" objects—a notion that implicitly gives credence to the reassuring idea that the designer, thoughtful and concerned about the well-being of all, devises remedies against the ills of civilization. To consider the murderer as a designer encourages us to challenge design's ongoing association with virtue by slightly changing the perspective and considering the discipline through the angle of its amorality.

Holmes is the contemporaneous antagonist of William Morris. While the latter partly rejected industrialization because he was wary of the consequences of the indiscriminate use of mechanization and feared that humans might no longer find a place in a world of machines, the former recognized its usefulness in the pursuit of his personal goals. The two figures mirror each other, each questioning from a different standpoint the relationship between morality and progress. This controversy extends beyond its historical framework, for design is rooted in a moral premise. What happens to it once it has been freed from this obligation?

It was precisely in the era of Morris, the good, and Holmes, the bad, that the discipline of design, modeled by an industrial and consumerist society, was established. It is impossible not to correlate the characteristics of modern urbanity at the end of the nineteenth century with those of today's cities, where the idea that the solution to all problems lies in curative or therapeutic morality is resurfacing, embodied by the figure of the thoughtful designer who is solely concerned with the well-being of all.

An industrial paradigm of rationalized performance, the Castle allowed Holmes to practice his art because, as one newspaper put it, "to him, murder was indeed a fine art, and he reveled in the lurid glamor cast upon him by his abnormal genius."[15] Art must here be understood in the broader sense of the aesthetic position defended by Thomas De Quincey, when he ventured to establish an unprecedented connection between the shadowy business of crime and that of the artist in "On Murder, Considered as One of the Fine Arts."[16] In this short story written in 1827, he imagines a gentleman's club called the Society of Connoisseurs in Murder, whose members, whom he describes as "Murder-Fanciers," debate the aesthetic merits of an a priori immoral and shocking activity.[17] De Quincey takes a counter-moral stance and invites his readers to adopt a different perspective: "We dry up our tears, and have the satisfaction, perhaps, to discover that a transaction, which, morally considered, was shocking and without a leg to stand upon, when tried by principles of Taste, turns out to be a very meritorius performance."[18]

In Fritz Lang's 1947 film *Secret Beyond the Door*, wealthy American heiress Celia Barrett marries Mark Lamphere, an architect whom she has just met in Mexico. Together they travel to Lavender Falls, Lamphere's family estate, where they settle in. A few days later, during their wedding reception, Lamphere shows their guests his strange collection of numbered rooms, which he explains to be reconstructions of rooms where famous murders have been committed. In room number one, for example, a sixteenth-century Catholic count supposedly killed his Huguenot wife accused of fomenting a plot; in room number two, a young man allegedly tied his mother to a chair during a flood in order to collect her life insurance. In yet another room, a replication of a scene from Paraguay, Don Ignacio reputedly killed his mistress with a rapier, according to the idea that "murder can be art too"—a paradoxical statement also uttered by one of the protagonists of Alfred Hitchcock's film *Rope* (released the following year), whose plot is loosely based on the seemingly unmotivated murder of a teenage boy by two students at the University of Chicago in 1924. Contrary to De Quincey, Hitchcock affirms that crime is crime and cannot be elevated to the rank of art; however, crime is a material that feeds into the work of art, in this case the film itself. So, while it may be problematic, if not unreasonable, to consider Holmes as an artist, he may legitimately claim his role as the designer and architect of the Castle, regardless of the fact that it was designed specifically to commit crimes.

It is precisely the serial and repetitive nature of Holmes's actions that, far from any reductive notion of "madness," motivated by profit rather than conviction or ideology, reveal the ugly face of capitalism, with industrial production its epitome, industrial design one of its manifestations, and the serial killer one of its states of production.

[1] "Confession of H. H. Holmes," 340.

[2] "Confession of H. H. Holmes."

[3] Giedion, *Space, Time and Architecture*, 9.

[4] Giedion, *Mechanization Takes Command*, 232.

[5] Giedion, 228.

[6] Sinclair, *Jungle*, 39.

[7] "The phenomenon of mechanized death will be regarded here neither from the sentimentalist's point of view nor from that of the food manufacturer. What interests us solely is the relation between mechanization and death," explains Giedion in *Mechanization Takes Command*, 240.

[8] Giedion, *Mechanization Takes Command*, 93. He goes on to note that, "for the speeding of output there was but one solution: to eliminate loss of time between each operation and the next, and to reduce the energy expended by the worker on the manipulation of heavy carcasses. In continuous flow, hanging from an endlessly moving chain at twenty-four-inch intervals, they now move in procession past a row of standing workers each of whom performs a single operation. Here was the birth of the model assembly line."

[9] See James Myles, *Chapters in the Life of a Dundee Factory Boy: An Autobiography* (Edinburgh: Adam and Charles Black, 1850). This is shown in the opening scene of *Metropolis* (1927) by Fritz Lang, where the workers' individuality makes way for a choreographed and elegantly cadenced entity of labor.

[10] Giedion, *Mechanization Takes Command*, 246.

[11] Giedion.

[12] *Chicago Times-Herald*, May 8, 1896, quoted in Schechter, *Depraved*, 278.

[13] Seltzer, *Serial Killers*, 204.

[14] Flusser, "About the Word *Design*," 20–21.

[15] *Chicago Daily News*, November 19, 1894, quoted in Jon Seidel, *Second City Sinners: True Crime from Historic Chicago's Deadly Streets* (Lanham, MD: Rowman and Littlefield, 2019), 40.

[16] Thomas De Quincey, "On Murder, Considered as One of the Fine Arts," *Blackwood's Magazine* (1827), https://www.gutenberg.org/files/10708/10708-8.txt.

[17] De Quincey.

[18] De Quincey.

Mr. Mudgett's Corpse Factory

When the little ghoul hired a secretary, his dark, watery eyes searched through her dress for qualifications not precisely clerical

BY BRADFORD D. JONES

IT NEVER OCCURRED to the Chicago police, nor to Amelia Cigrand's frantic parents, to look for her in the anatomy laboratory of the Hahnemann Medical School. Nor is it likely that they would have recognized her if they had, propped awkwardly as she was in one corner of the room. For Amelia was the class skeleton.

A pretty if naive 18-year-old, Amelia had arrived in Chicago in the spring of 1892, carrying $200 in her purse, a diploma from a secretarial school and romantically practical notions of finding a job where she could marry the boss. In Herman Webster Mudgett she found what she was looking for—or so she thought.

Mudgett, a clammy-handed little character dressed neatly in black, claimed to be a wealthy real estate operator. He had impressive offices on the third floor of his rambling, 37-room brick house at 701 63rd Street, and his glib speech and impeccable manners never failed to impress the droves of single women who answered his newspaper ads for investors. Actually, he lived entirely for—and by means of —sex, and as he sat beside the giant Franklin stove, interviewing Amelia for a job as a stenographer, his dark, watery eyes searched through her red velvet dress for qualifications not precisely secretarial.

Learning of her $200, Mudgett promptly hired her, and a few days later Amelia wrote her parents that Mr. Jackson, as she knew him, (*Continued on page 68*)

EYES BURNING, Mudgett walked toward Julia. He surveyed the awful work to be done with the logic of a madman.

Bradford D. Jones, "Mr. Mudgett's Corpse Factory," *Real: The Exciting Magazine*, January 19561956. Illustration by Raphael DeSoto.

Hounded To Death By Ghosts Of Castle He Built

Memory of Trap Doors, Secret Elevators and Stove, Wherein Bodies of Women Were Burned, Haunted Man for Nineteen Years.

UPPER LEFT — H. H. Holmes. Upper right —Holmes Castle. Below — Patrick Quinlan.

HOW ANIMALS AND BIRDS SLEEP

"Hounded to Death by Ghosts of Castle He Built," *Ogden Standard*, July 4, 1914. Courtesy of University of Utah, Marriott Library.

HOLMES CONFESSES 27 MURDERS

THE MOST AWFUL STORY OF MODERN TIMES TOLD BY THE FIEND IN HUMAN SHAPE.

Every Detail of His Fearful Crimes Told by the Man Who Admits He Is Turning Into the Shape of the Devil.

THE TALE OF THE GREATEST CRIMINAL IN HISTORY

The following statement was written by me in Philadelphia County Prison for the Philadelphia Inquirer as a true & accurate confession in all particulars. It is the only confession of my fearful crimes I have made or will make. I wrote it fully appreciating all the horrors it contains & how it condemns me before the world

Signed H H Holmes

Phila 9th 1896

HOLMES'
PRICE, 25 CENTS

OWN STORY

In which the Alleged Multi-Murderer and Arch conspirator tells of twenty-two Tragic deaths and disappearances

in which he is said to be Implicated, with Moyamensing Prison Diary Appendix

H. W. Mudgett M.D.

H. H. Holmes

ACCUSED OF MORE CRIMES THAN ANY OTHER MAN LIVING

PHILADELPHIA
BURK & McFETRIDGE CO.
1895

Front cover of *Holmes' Own Story*, by Herman W. Mudgett [H. H. Holmes, pseud.] (Philadelphia: Burk & McFetridge Co., 1895).

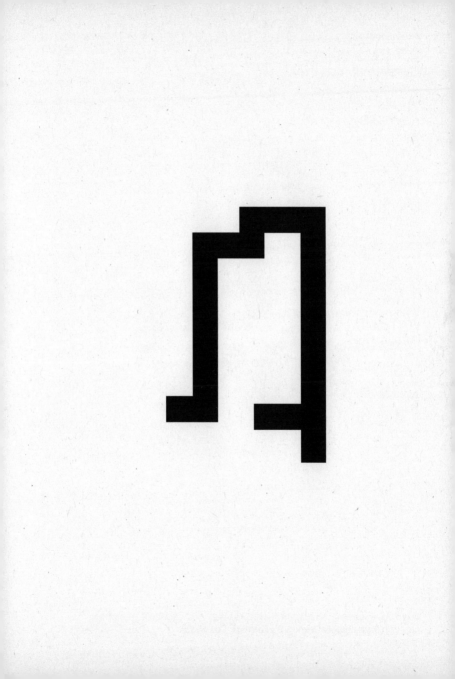

Alexandra Midal is an art and design historian who combines practice- and theory-based research as an artist-curator, writer, and film essayist. She is Professor in Design at the Master in Design – Space & Communication at HEAD – Geneva (Haute école d'arts appliqués)/HES-SO, and head of the Department of Critical Thinking at ENSCI (École nationale supérieure de création industrielle) in Paris.

She is the author of many books, including *Girls, The Troopers of Dance: Aesthetization of Politics and Manipulation of Entertainment* (Revue Faire, 2021), and *Design by Accident: For a New History of Design* (Sternberg Press, 2019), which revisits design history from the perspective of its struggles with visual arts and architecture, evolving around the concept of totality. Her writing about design and politics has featured in many books and catalogues, most recently in *Top secret. cinéma & espionage* (Flammarion, 2022). In addition to her writing, Midal has curated a number of exhibitions, including "Politique Fiction" at Cité du design, Saint-Étienne (2012–13) and "Tomorrow Now, When Design Meets Science Fiction" at MUDAM, Luxembourg City (2007).

Midal is also an experimental filmmaker and has shown some of her films (including *Shake, Shake, Shakers*; *Heaven is a State of Mind*; *Mind Player; Possessed*; *Home Sweet Ho(l)me(s)*; *Domestic Psycho; Hocus Pocus: Twilight in My Mind*; *Politique-Fiction*; *Eames, An Atlas*; and *Villa Frankenstein*) in the solo exhibition "Drive In"at CAPC, Museum of Contemporary Art, Bordeaux (2018–19) and in the group show "Au Bonheur" at CEAAC, Strasbourg (2022–23).

Domestic Psycho is a collection that infiltrates dark corners in art history and builds connections between visual and popular culture. Domestic Psycho zooms in on the unique, bizarre, and strange, taking as its starting point the idea that even if many of these extreme cases have gone unrecognized or uncatalogued, the scope of their contributions should not be dimished—quite the contrary, in fact. More amazing than fiction, these narratives form an astonishing portrait gallery which, by exploring marginal territories, speaks to the effects of the Industrial Revolution and technology on thought, art, and popular culture. If history's outcasts and dark corners have been marginalized for so long, embracing them today invites us to refresh, reformulate, and rethink the counter-figures, anti-heroes, and catalysts of a new history of the arts.

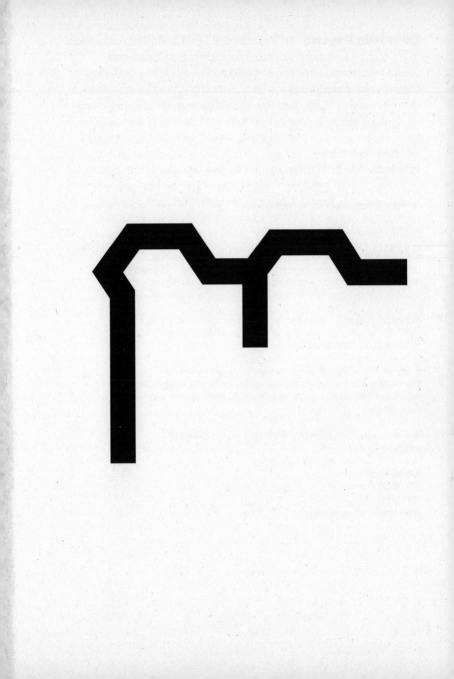

Alexandra Midal
The Murder Factory:
Life and Work of H. H. Holmes, First American Serial Killer

Published by Sternberg Press

Domestic Psycho I
Series editor: Alexandra Midal

Translator: Boris Kremer
Editor: Leah Whitman-Salkin
Proofreader: Raphael Wolf
Design: Rafaela Dražić
Printing: Tallinn Book Printers, Estonia

ISBN 978-3-95679-543-5

First published as *La manufacture du meurtre. Vie et oeuvre de
H. H. Holmes, premier serial killer américain* (Paris: Zones /
Éditions de la Découverte, 2018)

Distributed by The MIT Press, Art Data, Les presses du réel,
and Idea Books

Sternberg Press
71-75 Shelton Street
UK-London WC2H 9JQ
www.sternberg-press.com